UNNECESSARY WORDS

GIACOMO GIAMMATTEO

Inferno Publishing Company

Houston, TX

For more information about this book, visit my website.

Edition ISBNs

Trade Paperback 978-1-949074-85-7

E-book 978-1-949074-84-0

Book design by Giacomo Giammatteo

This edition was prepared by Giacomo Giammatteo gg@giacomog.com

❀ Formatted with Vellum

INTRODUCTION

Many people believe that good writing requires a large vocabulary, complicated sentences, and impressive language. And many writers assume that the more words they use, the more intelligent their writing will appear, but the opposite is usually true.

Strong writing depends on clarity. When readers have to plod through a book filled with unnecessary words, repeated ideas, vague language, and cluttered sentences, the message becomes harder to see. As a result, the reader spends more time deciphering the language than absorbing the idea.

Clear writing removes those obstacles.

This book examines one of the most common problems in writing: unnecessary words. Nearly every writer produces them. Some books will only have a few unnecessary words sprinkled among the pages, while others will be rife with them.

Wordy constructions appear in business reports, academic papers, emails, articles, and more. Almost every form of writing contains unnecessary words.

Often these words appear because writers repeat patterns they heard in conversation or saw in formal documents. Phrases such as *in order to, due to the fact that,* and *at this point in time* sound familiar, so writers slip them into their writing without much thought.

The problem is not that these expressions are grammatically incorrect — they just add length without adding meaning. When you use fewer words to say the same thing, readers understand the message more quickly, and the writing gains strength.

Other problems include hiding verbs inside nouns, filler words, redundant words, absolutes, and more. We'll cover each of them in more depth.

We'll also show that the goal isn't to shorten every sentence or remove every modifier. Some ideas require more words for explanation and detail.

The book also includes editing checklists, search strategies for locating wordy constructions, and practice exercises that allow readers to apply the principles right away. These tools help writers recognize patterns of unnecessary language and revise their work more efficiently.

Learning to remove unnecessary words is one of the most valuable skills a writer can develop. Once writers begin to recognize these patterns, they often discover that clarity improves quickly. Sentences become sharper, paragraphs become stronger, and ideas become easier to understand.

Good writing does not depend on using more words. It depends on choosing the right ones.

Think of Mark Twain's quote on using the right word: *"The difference between the right word and the almost right word is the difference between lightning and a lightning bug."*

Chapter One

WHY WRITERS USE TOO MANY WORDS

~~Most writers don't start out with the intention of writing wordy sentences.~~

Here's a tighter version of that sentence.

Most writers don't intend to write wordy sentences.

Wordiness rarely appears because writers ~~deliberately~~ choose to add extra language.

A better sentence deletes *deliberately*, as *choose* already implies intent.

We've only had two sentences. Let's look at them.

Most writers don't start out with the intention of writing wordy sentences. Wordiness rarely appears because writers deliberately choose to add extra language. (23 words)

The better option is below.

Most writers don't intend to write wordy sentences. Wordiness rarely appears because writers choose to add extra language. (18 words)

Eliminating the unnecessary words saves 5 words, but more importantly, it produces clearer sentences.

Unnecessary words usually appear in writing because certain habits are deeply embedded in the way people speak, and those habits transfer to their writing.

Spoken language often includes repeated phrases, filler words, and partial thoughts. When people speak, they pause, revise, and repeat ideas while searching for the right expression.

Listeners tolerate this because conversation moves quickly and context fills the gaps. But writing is different. Readers can't ask the writer to clarify a sentence. They need to understand the message the first time they see it. When you transfer conversational habits directly into writing, unnecessary words usually accompany those habits.

Another reason writers use too many words is that they believe longer sentences sound more intelligent. Students sometimes learn that academic writing should appear formal, and they conclude that formal writing requires longer sentences and complicated phrasing. This assumption leads them to replace clear words with longer expressions.

The committee made the decision to postpone the meeting.

This is a common sentence in corporate writing and emails.

The committee decided to postpone the meeting.

The sentence above shows the correct form.

The first version contains more words, but it doesn't communicate more meaning. Instead, it hides the main action inside a noun phrase. The verb *decided* becomes the phrase *made the decision.*

When writers turn verbs into nouns, sentences grow longer *and* weaker at the same time. The reader must work harder to find the action.

We'll cover this in more detail in the chapter on hidden verbs.

Chapter Two

QUIZ 1 & QUIZ ANSWERS

Revise each sentence to remove unnecessary words while preserving the meaning.

1. At this point in time the committee is currently reviewing the proposal.
2. The meeting lasted for two hours in total duration.
3. The team made a decision to postpone the project.
4. The reason why the system failed remains unclear.
5. The manager returned back to the office after lunch.
6. The company conducted an investigation of the accident.
7. It is important to note that the results show improvement.
8. The organization is in the process of implementing a new policy.
9. The project was delayed because of unexpected problems that were not anticipated.
10. The report contains several recommendations with regard to safety procedures.

Chapter 1 Quiz Answers

1. The committee is reviewing the proposal now.
2. The meeting lasted two hours.
3. The team decided to postpone the project.
4. The reason the system failed remains unclear.
5. The manager returned to the office after lunch.
6. The company investigated the accident.
7. The results show improvement.
8. The organization is implementing a new policy.
9. The project was delayed because of unexpected problems.
10. The report contains several recommendations about safety procedures.

Chapter Three

WORDY PHRASES THAT SHOULD DISAPPEAR

Some phrases appear so frequently in writing that you no longer notice them. These expressions sound normal because they are common in speech, reports, and academic writing. Unfortunately, many of them add words without adding meaning.

One of the most common examples is the phrase *in order to*. Don't make the mistake of believing that longer phrases sound more formal.

Look at the following sentence.

She left early *in order to* catch the train.

The phrase *in order to* contains three words, but only one of them is necessary. Removing the extra words produces a clearer sentence.

She left early to catch the train.

The meaning doesn't change, but the sentence is easier to read.

Another familiar phrase is *due to the fact that*. This expression appears frequently in academic papers and business reports, yet it rarely improves a sentence.

Take a look.

The game was cancelled *due to the fact* that it was raining.

The sentence is clearer when the phrase disappears.

The game was cancelled because it was raining.

Because expresses the same idea using fewer words.

Another example appears in the phrase *at this point in time*. Writers often use this expression when they want to refer to the present moment.

At this point in time we cannot make a decision.

The phrase contains five words, but a single word communicates the same idea.

We cannot make a decision now.

Shorter expressions allow readers to understand the sentence better.

Another phrase that appears frequently in reports is *for the purpose of*. Writers often use this construction when they want to describe an action or intention.

See for yourself.

The report was written *for the purpose of* explaining the problem.

The phrase *for the purpose of* adds unnecessary length. A clearer sentence removes the phrase entirely.

The report explains the problem.

The revised version communicates the same idea without extra wording. Longer phrases don't sound more precise. In most cases the opposite is true. Extra words often blur the meaning of the sentence rather than clarify it.

Another example appears in the phrase *in the event that*. Writers sometimes use this expression instead of the simpler word *if*.

Consider the following sentence.

In the event that the weather changes, the meeting will move indoors.

The sentence becomes clearer when the longer phrase disappears.

If the weather changes, the meeting will move indoors.

Both sentences communicate the same idea, but the shorter version reaches the point faster.

I can't think of any reason why you should use *in the event that* instead of *if* unless you're writing a novel and want a character to sound pedantic.

The phrase *with regard to* presents another example. Writers often believe this expression sounds more formal than about.

The report contains several recommendations *with regard to* safety procedures.

How about?

The report contains several recommendations *about* safety procedures.

Another phrase that frequently appears in writing is *the reason why*. Writers often include both words without realizing that the noun *reason* already contains the meaning of *why*.

Let's look at the dictionary definitions:

reason | ˈrēz(ə)n | noun

a cause, explanation, or justification for an action or event:

why | (h)wī | interrogative adverb

for what reason or purpose: *why did he do it?.*

The reason why the system failed remains unclear.

The word *why* adds nothing to the meaning of the sentence. A clearer version removes the unnecessary word.

The reason the system failed remains unclear.

Writers sometimes combine several wordy phrases in a single sentence. When this happens, the sentence becomes unnecessarily long.

. . .

At this point in time the committee is *in the process* of **reviewing the proposal.**

The sentence contains two wordy constructions. *At this point in time* and *in the process of* both add unnecessary length. A clearer version removes both phrases.

The committee is reviewing the proposal now.

Wordy phrases often survive because they sound familiar. We hear them repeatedly in professional environments, so we assume those phrases belong in formal writing. Clear writing depends on accuracy rather than tradition. If a shorter word communicates the idea clearly, the shorter word usually works better.

Another common example appears in the phrase *make a decision*. We often use this construction even though the verb *decide* expresses the same action.

The board will *make a decision* tomorrow.

The sentence becomes clearer when the verb appears directly.
The board will *decide* tomorrow.

The shorter version communicates the action immediately.
Similar patterns appear in many phrases.
***Conduct an investigation* becomes *investigate*.**
***Perform an analysis* becomes *analyze*.**
***Make a recommendation* becomes *recommend*.**
Each revision replaces a longer phrase with a direct verb.

These changes do more than shorten the sentence. They also strengthen it by placing the action where readers expect to find it.

. . .

Another phrase that often adds unnecessary length is *the fact that*. Writers sometimes insert this phrase when introducing a clause.

***The fact that* the project succeeded surprised everyone.**

The phrase *the fact that* adds two unnecessary words. The sentence becomes clearer when those words disappear.

The project's success surprised everyone.

The revised sentence expresses the same idea more directly.

Editing for wordy phrases requires attention to patterns. Writers should examine sentences that contain long expressions and ask whether shorter alternatives exist.

Readers appreciate writing that reaches the point quickly. Wordy phrases slow the reader because they delay the central idea of the sentence. When writers remove these phrases, the important information becomes easier to see.

The goal is not to eliminate every multiword phrase. Some expressions are necessary. The goal is to identify phrases that add length without adding meaning.

Writers who learn to recognize these patterns gain a powerful editing tool. Each time a wordy phrase disappears, the sentence becomes clearer.

The next chapter tackles another common source of wordiness — redundant expressions that repeat the same meaning.

Chapter Four

QUIZ 2 & QUIZ ANSWERS

Revise each sentence by removing wordy phrases.

1. She left early in order to catch the train.
2. The game was cancelled due to the fact that it was raining.
3. At this point in time we cannot make a decision.
4. The report was written for the purpose of explaining the problem.
5. In the event that the weather changes, the meeting will move indoors.
6. The board will make a decision tomorrow.
7. The team performed an analysis of the data.
8. The committee made a recommendation regarding the proposal.
9. The manager conducted an evaluation of the project.
10. The staff carried out an investigation of the complaint.

Chapter 2 Quiz Answers

1. She left early to catch the train.
2. The game was cancelled because it was raining.
3. We cannot make a decision now.
4. The report explains the problem.
5. If the weather changes, the meeting will move indoors.
6. The board will decide tomorrow.
7. The team analyzed the data.
8. The committee recommended changes to the proposal.
9. The manager evaluated the project.
10. The staff investigated the complaint.

Chapter Five

REDUNDANT EXPRESSIONS

Redundancy occurs when two words in a phrase express the same meaning. Writers use redundant phrases because the words sound familiar, but one of the words is always doing nothing.

Take the phrase *advance planning*. Planning always refers to something that happens ahead of time so the word advance adds no information.

Here's a definition for plan:

verb (**plans**) (, **planning** | planiNG |) (, **planned** | pland |) *[with object]*

decide on and arrange in advance:

Redundancies show up everywhere — on résumés, in cover letters, job descriptions, emails, proposals, contracts, and yes, books. Most redundancies are harmless, but they weaken your writing. Removing them tightens every sentence they touch.

Why It Matters
One of the most sought-after traits in any professional setting is

the ability to communicate clearly and concisely. Eliminating redundancies is a direct path to that. Once you learn to spot them, you will see and hear them constantly — in meetings, on TV, and in print. The more you recognize them, the harder it becomes to use them without noticing.

Redundant phrases survive because they sound natural. You absorb them from conversation and reproduce them automatically. But careful readers notice that the extra word contributes nothing. During revision, those words need to go.

Common Patterns

Before the full list, it helps to understand the patterns redundancies follow. Most fall into one of these categories.

Verbs that already contain their direction

Some verbs have a built-in direction, making any directional modifier pointless. Fall already means downward. Lift already means upward. Drop can only go one way. If you fall, no one pictures you falling up to the ceiling. Examples: fall (down), lift (up), drop (down), rise (up), raise (up), sit (down), stand (up), kneel (down).

Acronyms with a repeated word

Many acronyms include a word that people then repeat aloud. The M in ATM stands for machine, so "ATM machine" says machine twice. The same applies to PIN number (N = number), RAM memory (M = memory), HIV virus (V = virus), ISBN number (N = number), LCD display (D = display), UPC code (C = code), and GOP Party (P = party).

So it's ATM, not ATM machine. It's PIN, not PIN number, etc.

Words whose modifier is already in the definition

Some nouns and verbs contain their apparent modifiers inside their definitions. A result is the end, so "end result" is redundant. A conclusion is final, so "final conclusion" repeats itself. An emergency is unexpected by nature. A fad is passing. A haven is safe. A breakthrough is major. The list is long. We'll go into more detail on all of these later.

Verbs meaning "to bring together"

A family of verbs already means to join things: blend, collaborate, combine, connect, gather, join, merge, and splice. Adding "together" to any of them is unnecessary. You do not blend something apart.

"New" words that are already new

Several nouns are new by definition. An *innovation* is a new thing or method. An *invention* is something that has never been made or used before. A *beginning* is the start. A *recruit* is new. Putting "new" in front of any of them repeats the obvious.

"Past" words that are already in the past

Experience is in the past — you cannot have experience with something you have not yet done. *History* is the past. *Memories* are the past. *Records* are things that were recorded, placing them firmly in the past. Saying "past experience" or "past history" adds nothing.

The List

The words in parentheses are the unnecessary ones. Entries that share the same explanation are grouped together.

A

(Absolutely) necessary — Necessary means essential — something you cannot do without. Something either is or is not necessary. "Absolutely" adds no information.

(Actual) facts — A fact is something known to be true. "Actual" repeats the definition.

Add an (additional) — "Add" and "additional" mean the same thing. Use one. "I would like to add an order of fries" and "I would like an additional order of fries" are the same sentence.

(Added) bonus — A bonus is by definition something added. No need to say so.

Adequate (enough) — Adequate means sufficient for the need. Enough means the same thing.

(Advance) warning — A warning is given in advance. That is the entire point of a warning.

(All-time) record — If someone sets a record, it is already *all-time* by definition.

(Already) existing — If something exists, it is already in existence.

(And) etc. — Etc. is Latin for "and so forth." Adding "and" before it makes it "and and so forth."

(Armed) gunman — A gunman is already armed with a gun.

(Artificial) prosthesis — A prosthesis is defined as an artificial body part. The word artificial is in the definition.

ATM (machine) — The M stands for machine.

At the present time / (Present) time — Just say "now."

Autobiography (of his or her own life) — An autobiography is your own life story, told by you. Saying it is all that is necessary.

B

Bald (headed) — Bald refers to the head. A bald eagle does not refer to its tail.

Balsa (wood) — Balsa is the South American tree from which balsa comes. Since balsa is wood, there is no need to say so. Saying "balsa wood" is like saying "oak wood."

(Basic) fundamentals — Fundamentals are basic. That is what the word means.

Best (ever) — If it is the best, it is already better than everything that came before it.

Biography (of his or her life) — A biography is an account of someone's life. "Of his or her life" is built into the definition.

(Blatantly) obvious — Blatantly means you are not hiding it — in other words, you are being obvious.

Blend / Combine / Connect / Gather / Join / Merge / Splice (together) — All these verbs already mean to bring things together. You do not blend something apart. So, you don't blend together, connect together, gather together, join together, etc.; you simply blend, connect, gather, or join.

Bouquet (of flowers) — A bouquet is an arrangement of flowers. "He sent me a bouquet" is all you need.

(Brief) moment — A moment is brief. A long moment is not a moment.

(Brief) summary — A summary is brief by definition.

Browse (through) — To browse means to look through.

(Burning) embers — An ember is defined as the burning remnant of a fire.

C

Cancel (out) — You simply cancel. You do not cancel out or cancel in.

(Careful) scrutiny — Scrutiny is the act of carefully examining something.

Cease (and desist) — Desist means to cease. They are the same word.

Circle (around) — To circle something is to go around it.

(Close) proximity — Proximity already means nearness. "He was in close proximity" is like saying "he was close close to it."

(Closed) fist — To make a fist means to close your hand.

(Completely) annihilate / destroy / eliminate / engulf / fill / surround — All these verbs imply totality. Annihilate means to utterly destroy. Surround means to be all the way around. Completely is built into each of them.

Compete (with each other) — To compete already implies that others are trying to win the same thing.

Consensus (of opinion) — Consensus means everyone has agreed. "Of opinion" is redundant.

(Constantly) maintained — Maintained means to keep something without change. Constantly is implied.

Convicted felon — A felon is someone who has been convicted of a serious crime. Convicted is in the definition.

Could (possibly) — Could already expresses possibility. He either could or he could not.

Crisis (situation) — The definition of crisis includes the word situation.

(Critically) important — Important means it is critical.

(Current) trend — A trend is, by definition, current.

Currently away (or unavailable) — "I'm away from my desk" is all that is needed. "Currently" and "right now" are both redundant. The triple redundancy "I'm currently away from my desk right now" is the worst version of this.

Currently is one of the few words that I feel we could do without. There is almost never a time when it's needed.

D

(Different) kinds — Kinds are, by definition, different from one another.

Drop (down) — There is nowhere else to drop but down.

During (the course of) — During means "in the course of." The two phrases are identical.

E

Each (and every) — Use each or every, but not both. "I gave a dollar to each child" and "I gave a dollar to every child" mean the same thing.

Earlier (in time) — Earlier already refers to time.

(Early) beginnings — Beginnings are the beginning. You cannot get earlier than that.

(Empty) hole / (Empty) space — A hole is a hollow space by definition. Space refers to an empty or available area. Both are already empty.

Emergency (situation) — An emergency is already a situation. If you knew it was coming, you could prepare, and it would not be an emergency.

Enclosed (herein) — Herein means within this document, and enclosed means enclosed. No need for both.

(End) result / (Final) conclusion / (Final) end / (Final) outcome — A result is the end. A conclusion is final. An outcome is final. In each case, the modifier simply restates what the noun already means.

Enter (in) — To enter is to go in.

Equal (to one another) — Equal already implies a comparison between two or more things.

(Exact) same — Exact means the same. "They're exactly the same" and "they're the same" are identical.

Evolve (over time) — Evolve implies a gradual change over time. Evolution does not happen instantaneously.

F

(Face) mask — A mask is worn on the face. No one wears an arm mask or a leg mask.

Fall (down) — Where else do you fall?

(False) pretenses — A pretense involves deceiving. It is always false.

(Favorable) approval — Approval implies a favorable response.

(First and) foremost — Foremost means most prominent. Adding "first" repeats the idea.

(First) conceived — To conceive, meaning to think up, already implies it is the first time.

First (of all) — "First" is sufficient. "First of all, let me say this" adds nothing over "first, let me say this."

Fly (through the air) — Where else would you fly?

(Foreign) imports — Imports are, by definition, foreign. If they are not from abroad, they are not imports.

(Former) graduate — If you are a graduate, it is already in the past. You are not a *former* graduate — you are a graduate.

(Free) gift — A gift is free. Otherwise it is a purchase.

(From) whence — Whence means "from which" or "from where." Adding "from" is like saying "from from where."

(Frozen) ice — Ice is frozen water.

Full (to capacity) — Capacity means the maximum amount. If it is full, it is at capacity.

(Future) plans — Plans are forward-looking by definition. You do not plan the past.

G–H

(General) public — Public and general share the same meaning in this context.

GOP (Party) — GOP stands for Grand Old Party.

(Had done) previously — If you "had done" something, it was done in the past — previously.

(Head) honcho — Honcho already implies leader or top person.

HIV (virus) — The V stands for virus.

(Hollow) tube — A tube is hollow by definition.

Hourly / weekly / yearly (basis) — No need for "basis." "She did the laundry weekly" is sufficient on its own.

Hurry (up) — There is no meaningful difference between "hurry" and "hurry up."

I–K

(Illustrated) drawing — Illustrated already implies the presence of drawings.

Incredible (to believe) — Incredible means not credible — difficult to believe. "Incredible to believe" is like saying "difficult to believe to believe."

Indicted (on a charge) — Indicted means charged.

Interdependent (on each other) — Interdependent means mutually dependent on each other. "On each other" is built in.

Introduced (anew) / Introduced (for the first time) — To introduce means to bring something to others' attention for the first time. Both modifiers repeat the definition.

(Ir)regardless — "Ir" means not, and regardless means without regard. Together they cancel each other out. Use regardless.

ISBN (number) — The N stands for number.

(Joint) collaboration — Collaboration means to work jointly with others. "Joint" repeats it.

Kneel (down) — You kneel on the floor. You do not kneel on the ceiling.

(Knowledgeable) experts — If they are experts, one would hope they are knowledgeable.

L–M

Lag (behind) — To lag means to fall behind. You do not lag ahead.

Later (time) — Later alone is sufficient.

LCD (display) — The D stands for display.

Lift (up) — You would not lift something down.

Made (out) of — Say "made of" or "made from." "Made out of" is unnecessary.

(Major) breakthrough — A breakthrough is, by definition, major.

Meet (with each other) — Meet already implies more than one person is involved.

(Mental) telepathy — Telepathy is mind reading. Mental is implied.

Might (possibly) — Might already expresses the possibility of something.

N–O

(Native) habitat — A habitat is the natural environment of an organism. Native is included in the concept.

(Natural) instinct — Instinct is what you do naturally, without having to think about it.

Never (before) — If it was never, then it was not before, either.

(New) beginning / innovation / invention / recruit — All these nouns are new by definition. A beginning is new. An innovation is a new thing or method. An invention has never been made before. A recruit is new.

Nothing / None (at all) — Nothing means nothing. "At all" adds nothing.

(Number one) leader — If you are the leader, you are number one. Leader implies it.

Off (of) — "Get off the couch," not "get off of the couch."

(Old) adage / cliché / custom / proverb — All these words already imply age. An adage is old. A cliché is overused, meaning it has been around for a long time. A custom and a proverb carry the same implication.

(Open) trench — A trench is open by definition.

Outside (of) — "Outside" alone is sufficient.

(Over) exaggerate — Exaggerate already means to overstate.

(Overused) cliché — Cliché means overused.

. . .

P

(Pair of) twins — Twins are, by definition, a pair of two.

Palm (of the hand) — Where else would the palm be?

(Passing) fad — A fad is short-lived by nature.

(Past) experience / history / memories / records — All four words already refer to the past. Experience is something you have already done. History is the past. Memories are the past. Records are things that were recorded.

Period (of time) — A period is of time. If not, then a period of what?

(Personal) friend / opinion — Both are personal by definition. If it is not your personal opinion, whose opinion is it?

Pick (and choose) — Pick and choose mean the same thing. Use one.

PIN (number) — The N stands for number.

Plan (ahead) — Same as future plans. Plans are, by definition, ahead.

Please RSVP — RSVP is French for "please respond."

(Polar) opposites — "Opposites" alone is sufficient.

(Positive) identification — To identify someone means you are positive who it is.

Postpone (until later) — To postpone is to put something off until later.

Pouring (down) rain — Rain comes down. Wind may carry it sideways briefly, but it is coming down.

(Pre)board — To board means to get onto something. You cannot get on before you get on.

(Pre)record — You cannot record something before you record it. "Pre" is built into the act itself.

Proof (positive) — Proof means you are positive. "The detective had proof she committed the crime."

Protest (against) — A protest is an action against something. There is no need to add "against."

. . .

R

Raise (up) — Raise means to move to a higher position. If you are not raising up, where are you raising?

RAM (memory) — The M stands for memory.

Reason is (because) — A reason is a cause or justification. "The reason is because" is a circular construction.

Reason (why) — "Reason" alone is sufficient. There is no difference between "what was the reason he did it" and "why he did it."

(Regular) routine — A routine is a sequence of actions performed regularly.

Revert (back) — To revert means to go back.

Rise (up) — You can only rise up.

S

(Safe) haven — A haven is a safe place. You have never heard of an unsafe haven.

(Sand) dune — A dune is a hill of sand near the ocean or in a desert.

(Serious) danger — Danger is serious.

(Sharp) point — A point is described as the sharp end of a tool or pencil. Sharpness is implied.

Sit (down) / Stand (up) — The directions are implied by both verbs.

Skipped (over) — Just "skipped."

(Slight) edge — When used to mean an advantage, edge already implies something slight.

Spell out (in detail) — "Spell out" means to provide detail.

Start (off / out) — "Start" alone is sufficient.

(Steady) stream — A stream is a steady flow of something.

Sufficient (enough) — Sufficient is enough.

(Sum) total — To sum something is to total it.

Surrounded (on all sides) — Surround means to be all the way around something.

(Sworn) affidavit — An affidavit is sworn testimony.

T

(Temper) tantrum — A tantrum is a fit of temper.

Three a.m. (in the morning) — A.m. is the morning.

(Three-way) love triangle — A triangle has three sides. "Love triangle" says it all.

(Total) destruction — Destruction is total.

(True) facts — Facts are true by definition. That is why they are called facts.

(Truly) sincere — Sincere means true.

(Two equal) halves — Halves are equal by definition. If they were not equal, they would not be halves.

Tuna (fish) — A tuna is a fish. We do not say "salmon fish" or "chicken fowl."

Twelve noon / midnight — Noon and midnight already mean twelve o'clock.

U–W

(Underground) subway — A subway is an underground railroad.

(Unexpected) emergency — If you knew it was coming, you could prepare, and it would not be an emergency.

(Unexpected) surprise — A surprise is, by definition, unexpected.

(Unintentional) mistake — Mistakes are unintentional. No one makes a mistake on purpose.

UPC (code) — The C stands for code.

(Very) pregnant — You are either pregnant or you are not.

(Very) unique — Unique means one of a kind. It cannot come in degrees.

Visible (to the eye) — Visible means capable of being seen. Do you prefer things visible to the ear?

(Wall) mural — The definition of mural indicates its location.

Warn (in advance) — A warning is given in advance of something happening. That is its entire purpose.

A Note on "Pre"

The prefix "pre" works well with nouns and points in time: presale, prewar, pre-Caesar. It does not work well with action verbs. Pre-board, pre-record, and pre-order all describe doing something before you do that same thing — which is logically impossible. We understand what is meant, but understanding something does not make it right.

When It May Not Be Redundant

Before labeling something redundant, make certain it is. Consider boiling hot and freezing cold. The argument against them is that if something is boiling, it is hot, and if it is freezing, it is cold. That is fair. But boiling and freezing can also function as adjectives describing degree — not just hot or cold, but *hot enough to boil water, cold enough to freeze*. In that reading, they add meaning.

Context matters. If the words are being used simply to reinforce that something is hot or cold, they are redundant. If they are describing degree, they are not. The same principle applies before declaring anything on this list redundant in a specific context. When in doubt, ask whether the second word adds anything the first does not already contain.

Another example: arm's reach. Reach can mean many things — communicating with someone, the reach of the law, an area of influence. When arm specifies the physical type of reach, it earns its place.

Chapter Six

CHAPTER 3 & QUIZ ANSWERS

Remove redundant words.

1. The team completed the project in close proximity to the deadline.
2. The investigation revealed the true facts about the incident.
3. Please return back to your seat.
4. The committee combined together several reports.
5. The final outcome of the study surprised everyone.
6. The manager made advance plans for the meeting.
7. The policy was completely finished before the review.
8. The report summarizes and gives an overview of the results.
9. The proposal included several basic fundamentals of the plan.
10. The software failed because of an unexpected error that the team did not expect.

Chapter 3 Quiz Answers

1. The team completed the project near the deadline.
2. The investigation revealed the facts about the incident.
3. Please return to your seat.
4. The committee combined several reports.
5. The outcome of the study surprised everyone.
6. The manager planned the meeting in advance.
7. The policy was finished before the review.
8. The report summarizes the results.
9. The proposal included several fundamentals of the plan.
10. The software failed because of an unexpected error.

Chapter Seven

FILLER WORDS THAT WEAKEN WRITING

Many sentences contain words that add emphasis but contribute little meaning. These words often appear when you want to sound conversational or expressive. In practice, they usually weaken the sentence instead of strengthening it.

Common filler words include *actually, basically, really, very, quite, rather,* and *somewhat.* You'll find you often insert these words automatically, and not only don't you notice them when you write, but you don't notice them when you edit.

Look at a few here:

The meeting was actually very important.

The word *actually* adds no useful meaning. Removing it strengthens the sentence.

The meeting was very important.

Even the word *very* may be unnecessary. A stronger revision removes both filler words.

The meeting was important.

Another example is the word *really*. Writers often use this word when they want to intensify an adjective.

The results were really surprising.

The word *really* attempts to increase emphasis, but removing the word makes the sentence stronger.

The results were surprising.

If greater emphasis is necessary, a more precise adjective usually works better than a filler word.

Here's another example.

The results were very good.

The phrase *very good* communicates only a general idea. Replacing the phrase with a more precise word produces a clearer sentence.

The results were excellent.

The revision removes the filler word and replaces it with a stronger adjective. Filler words often appear when you hesitate. Words such as *perhaps*, *maybe*, or *sort of* sometimes appear when you feel uncertain about the statement.

These words can be useful when genuine uncertainty exists, but they often appear even when you intend to make a clear claim.

Consider this.

The new policy is *sort of* effective.

The phrase *sort of* weakens the statement without clarifying the meaning. A stronger sentence removes the filler phrase.

The new policy is effective.

If you wish to express uncertainty, the sentence should describe that uncertainty more clearly.

The new policy *appears* to be effective.

The revision explains the writer's meaning without relying on vague filler language.

Another filler word that appears frequently in speech and writing is *basically*. Writers sometimes use this word when summarizing an idea.

Consider the following sentence.

The plan *basically* solves the problem.

The word *basically* adds little meaning. A clearer sentence removes the filler word.

The plan solves the problem.

Writers also use the word *quite* as a form of emphasis. Unfortunately, the word often creates confusion because its meaning changes depending on context.

The proposal is *quite* interesting.

The word *quite* may mean very, somewhat, or simply interesting depending on how the reader interprets it. Removing the word produces a clearer statement.

The proposal is interesting.

Another example involves the word *rather*. Writers sometimes use this word to soften criticism or disagreement.

The report is *rather* confusing.

The word *rather* weakens the statement without improving clarity.

The report is confusing.

The revised sentence communicates the idea more directly.

Filler words sometimes appear in clusters. Writers may combine several emphasis words without realizing how much they weaken the sentence.

Consider the following example.

The results were *actually really very* surprising.

The sentence contains three filler words. Each one attempts to increase emphasis, but together they create unnecessary clutter. A clearer sentence removes the extra words.

The results were surprising.

The revision communicates the same idea in a much cleaner form.

One reason filler words survive in writing is that they rarely change the basic meaning of the sentence. Because the sentence still makes sense, the writer may not notice the problem during revision. Reading sentences aloud can reveal these unnecessary words. When writers hear the rhythm of the sentence, filler words often sound awkward or excessive.

The explanation was *actually quite* helpful.

The sentence becomes stronger when the filler words disappear.

The explanation was helpful.

The meaning remains the same, but the sentence becomes more direct.

If you worry that removing filler words will make your writing sound harsh — don't. In most cases the opposite happens. Clear sentences feel confident and precise.

When you rely on strong verbs and precise nouns, you rarely need filler words to strengthen the sentence. Meaning becomes clearer because the sentence depends on accurate language rather than unnecessary emphasis.

Recognizing filler words is an important editing skill. You should examine sentences that contain words such as *actually, really, very,* or *basically* and ask whether those words contribute meaning.

The next chapter examines another pattern that produces unnecessary language — weak openings that delay the subject of the sentence.

Chapter Eight

CHAPTER 4 & QUIZ ANSWERS

Remove filler words.

1. The meeting was actually very important.
2. The results were really surprising.
3. The plan basically solves the problem.
4. The proposal is quite interesting.
5. The report is rather confusing.
6. The results were actually really very surprising.
7. The explanation was actually quite helpful.
8. The manager spoke very clearly during the meeting.
9. The results were very good.
10. The solution was extremely important to the project.

Chapter 4 Quiz Answers

1. The meeting was important.
2. The results were surprising.
3. The plan solves the problem.
4. The proposal is interesting.
5. The report is confusing.
6. The results were surprising.
7. The explanation was helpful.
8. The manager spoke clearly during the meeting.
9. The results were excellent.
10. The solution was essential to the project.

Chapter Nine

WEAK OPENINGS THAT DELAY THE SENTENCE

Many sentences begin with language that delays the real subject. These openings often appear harmless, but they push the main idea farther into the sentence than necessary. Readers must pass through extra words before reaching the meaning.

One of the most common weak openings begins with the phrase *there is* or *there are.* Writers often use these constructions without noticing them.

Examples follow.

There are several factors that influence the success of a project.

The sentence begins with *there are,* which adds no meaning. The real subject of the sentence is several factors, so a clearer sentence removes the unnecessary opening.

Several factors influence a project's success.

The revised sentence moves the subject forward and reaches the point more quickly.

A second example shows the same pattern.

There are many writers who struggle with unnecessary words.

The phrase *there are* delays the subject of the sentence. Removing the weak opening produces a stronger version.

Many writers struggle with unnecessary words.

The sentence becomes more direct because the subject appears immediately.

People sometimes believe that the phrase *there is* helps introduce an idea gently. In practice it usually weakens the sentence. Readers prefer sentences that move directly to the subject.

Here's another example.

***There is* a possibility that the meeting will be postponed.**

The phrase *there is* a possibility delays the real point of the sentence.

The meeting may be postponed.

The revision communicates the same idea with greater clarity.

Another weak construction begins with the phrase *it is*. Writers often use this structure when introducing a statement.

Consider the following example.

***It is* important to recognize unnecessary words during editing.**

The phrase *it is* delays the real subject of the sentence. A clearer version removes the weak opening.

Recognizing unnecessary words during editing is important.

The revision places the subject at the beginning of the sentence. Writers frequently combine *it is* with longer expressions such as *it is important to note that* or *it should be noted that*. These phrases usually introduce statements that do not require any introduction.

Consider the following.

***It should be noted that* the report contains several errors.**

The phrase *it should be noted that* adds several unnecessary words. Removing the phrase produces a clearer sentence.

The report contains several errors.

Another weak opening appears in the phrase *there is no doubt that*. Writers sometimes use this expression to emphasize certainty.

***There is no doubt that* the decision was difficult.**

The decision was difficult.

You saved four words and improved the sentence.

Weak openings also appear when writers begin sentences with phrases such as *it seems that, it appears that,* or *it is possible that.* These expressions sometimes indicate uncertainty, but they often appear even when you intend to make a direct statement.

It appears that the system failed during testing.

If you are confident about the conclusion, the sentence should say so clearly.

The system failed during testing.

If you want to express uncertainty, the sentence should do so directly.

The system may have failed during testing.

Both revisions communicate the idea more clearly than the original sentence.

Another weak opening appears in the phrase *the fact that.* Writers often use this construction when introducing an idea.

The fact that the project succeeded surprised everyone.

The phrase *the fact that* adds unnecessary length.

The project's success surprised everyone.

Writers sometimes combine several weak openings in a single sentence. When this happens, the sentence becomes unnecessarily long. Consider the following example.

There are several reasons why the project failed.

The sentence contains two unnecessary elements. The phrase *there are* delays the subject, and the phrase the *reason why* contains redundancy.

A clearer version removes both problems.

Several reasons explain the project's failure.

The revision places the subject at the beginning and removes unnecessary wording.

Weak openings slow the reader because they delay the main idea. Readers prefer sentences that reach the subject and verb quickly. When the subject appears early, the meaning becomes easier to follow.

During revision writers should examine the beginning of each sentence. If a sentence begins with phrases such as *there is, there are, it is,* or *it should be noted that,* the writer should consider whether the sentence can begin more directly.

In many cases the sentence becomes stronger when the unnecessary opening disappears. Clear writing allows the reader to see the idea immediately. Removing weak openings helps achieve that goal.

The next chapter examines another pattern that produces unnecessary words — constructions that hide verbs inside longer phrases.

Chapter Ten

CHAPTER 5 & QUIZ ANSWERS

Rewrite the sentences to remove weak openings.

1. There are many factors that influence success.
2. There is a possibility that the meeting will be cancelled.
3. It is important to understand the policy changes.
4. There are several reasons why the project failed.
5. It should be noted that the report contains errors.
6. There are many writers who struggle with wordiness.
7. It appears that the system failed during testing.
8. There are several issues that require attention.
9. It is possible that the policy will change.
10. There are many examples that illustrate this problem.

Chapter 5 Quiz Answers

1. Many factors influence success.
2. The meeting may be cancelled.
3. Understanding the policy changes is important.
4. Several reasons explain the project's failure.
5. The report contains errors.
6. Many writers struggle with wordiness.
7. The system failed during testing.
8. Several issues require attention.
9. The policy may change.
10. Many examples illustrate this problem.

Chapter Eleven

HIDDEN VERBS AND NOMINALIZATIONS

Another common source of unnecessary words appears when writers turn verbs into nouns. This process is called nominalization. A verb that normally expresses action becomes a noun, and the sentence must then add extra words to support it. The result is usually a longer and weaker sentence.

Writers often do this without noticing it. In everyday speech people sometimes convert verbs into nouns because the phrasing sounds formal or official. When that habit enters writing, sentences grow heavier and less direct.

Look at this sentence.

The committee *made a decision* to postpone the meeting.

The noun *decision* comes from the verb *decide*. Because the action appears as a noun, the sentence must add the phrase *made a* and the sentence becomes longer than necessary. A clearer version restores the verb.

The committee *decided* to postpone the meeting.

The revision removes two unnecessary words and places the action where readers expect to find it.

Another example shows the same pattern.

The company *conducted an investigation* of the accident.

The noun *investigation* comes from the verb *investigate*. The sentence adds the phrase conducted an to support the noun. A clearer version restores the verb.

The company *investigated* the accident.

Nominalizations appear frequently in professional writing. Many reports contain phrases such as *make a recommendation, conduct an analysis,* or *perform an evaluation.* Each phrase hides a verb inside a longer construction.

Consider the following sentence.

The team *performed an analysis* of the available data.

The noun analysis comes from the verb *analyze.* Because the verb has been converted into a noun, the sentence must include the phrase performed an. A clearer version restores the verb.

The team *analyzed* the available data.

The revised sentence removes unnecessary words and highlights the action.

Another example appears in the phrase *make a recommendation.*

The committee will *make a recommendation* tomorrow.

The noun *recommendation* comes from the verb recommend. A clearer sentence restores the verb.

The committee will *recommend* a solution tomorrow.

Nominalizations often appear together with weak verbs such as *make, conduct, perform,* or *carry out.* These verbs support the noun that contains the real action.

The department *carried out an* evaluation of the policy.

The noun evaluation comes from the verb *evaluate.* The sentence becomes clearer when the verb returns to its original form.

The department *evaluated* the policy.

Writers sometimes believe that nominalizations sound more formal or professional, but sentences that hide verbs often sound bureaucratic and difficult to read. Readers prefer sentences in which the action appears clearly. When verbs remain verbs, the sentence moves forward with energy.

Another example.

The organization *made an announcement* about the new policy.

The noun *announcement* comes from the verb *announce*. The phrase *made an announcement* adds unnecessary words.

The organization *announced* the new policy.

Another example illustrates how nominalizations can accumulate in a single sentence.

The committee *conducted an evaluation* and *made a recommendation* regarding the proposal.

Both *evaluation* and *recommendation* hide verbs. The sentence must add several words to support them.

A clearer version restores the verbs.

The committee *evaluated* the proposal and *recommended* changes.

Nominalizations also appear when writers combine nouns with prepositional phrases. This structure often produces sentences that feel heavy and indirect.

The *implementation* of the new system required the *completion* of several tests.

The sentence contains two nominalizations. The nouns *implementation* and *completion* come from the verbs *implement* and *complete*.

***Implementing* the new system required *completing* several tests.**

Another example shows how several nominalizations can appear together.

The *investigation* led to the *discovery* of several errors in the report.

The nouns *investigation* and *discovery* both hide verbs.

A clearer version restores the verbs.

Investigating the report _revealed_ several errors.

Writers sometimes rely on nominalizations because they appear frequently in technical or administrative language. Legal documents, government reports, and corporate memoranda often contain long strings of noun phrases. While those constructions may seem official, they usually reduce clarity, and readers must search through the sentence to find the action.

Clear writing places the action in the verb.

Another useful editing strategy is to look for nouns that end with common nominalization endings such as _-tion, -ment, -ance,_ or _-ity._ Many of these nouns come from verbs.

Examples include _implementation, development, assessment,_ and _evaluation._

Not every noun with these endings should disappear. Some nouns express ideas that cannot easily become verbs. However, you should examine these words carefully during revision.

The _development_ of the proposal required several revisions.

The noun _development_ comes from the verb _develop._ The sentence becomes clearer when the verb appears directly.

Developing the proposal required several revisions.

Another example appears in the noun assessment.

The committee _performed an_ assessment of the project.

The committee _assessed_ the project.

The revision removes unnecessary words and strengthens the sentence.

Recognizing nominalizations requires attention during editing. You should look for phrases that contain weak verbs combined with abstract nouns. These combinations often hide the real action of the sentence.

When you restore the verb, sentences become shorter and clearer.

Readers can identify the action immediately, which improves both clarity and rhythm.

The goal is not to eliminate every noun that comes from a verb, but some nouns perform useful functions in a sentence. The goal is to recognize when a verb has been hidden unnecessarily.

Clear writing depends on strong verbs. When verbs carry the action of the sentence, the language becomes more direct and more precise.

The next chapter examines another pattern that produces unnecessary language — long chains of prepositional phrases that add words without improving meaning.

Chapter Twelve

CHAPTER 6 & QUIZ ANSWERS

Revise each sentence by restoring the hidden verb and removing unnecessary words.

1. The committee made a recommendation regarding the policy change.
2. The company conducted an investigation of the complaint.
3. The team performed an analysis of the available data.
4. The department carried out an evaluation of the program.
5. The manager made an announcement about the new schedule.
6. The organization made improvements in the area of communication.
7. The staff completed the implementation of the new procedure.
8. The board conducted a review of the proposal.
9. The committee made a decision to delay the vote.
10. The company performed an assessment of the project.

Chapter 6 Quiz Answers

1. The committee recommended a policy change.
2. The company investigated the complaint.
3. The team analyzed the available data.
4. The department evaluated the program.
5. The manager announced the new schedule.
6. The organization improved communication.
7. The staff implemented the new procedure.
8. The board reviewed the proposal.
9. The committee decided to delay the vote.
10. The company assessed the project.

Chapter Thirteen

PREPOSITIONAL OVERLOAD

Prepositions are small words that connect ideas. Words such as *of, in, for, with, to,* and *from* help show relationships between parts of a sentence. These words are necessary in many situations, but sentences sometimes contain so many prepositions that the meaning becomes difficult to follow.

When writers rely heavily on prepositional phrases, sentences often grow longer without becoming clearer. The reader must move through several layers of language before reaching the main point.

The results *of the analysis of the data from the experiment* were surprising.

The sentence contains several prepositional phrases. The phrases *of the analysis, of the data,* and *from the experiment* appear in a chain that slows the reader. Let's simplify the structure.

The experimental data produced surprising results.

Another example illustrates the same pattern.

The discussion *of the proposal in the meeting with the committee* lasted two hours.

The sentence contains multiple prepositional phrases. The reader must pass through *of the proposal, in the meeting,* and *with the committee* before reaching the main idea.

A clearer sentence simplifies the structure.

The committee *discussed* the proposal for two hours.

The revised version replaces several prepositional phrases with a strong verb. Prepositional overload often occurs when writers rely on nouns instead of verbs.

Nouns frequently require additional phrases to explain their meaning. Verbs usually express the same idea more directly.

The completion *of the project by the team* occurred *before the deadline.*

The sentence contains several prepositional phrases. The phrases *of the project, by the team,* and *before the deadline* create a long structure.

A clearer sentence restores the verb.

The team completed the project before the deadline.

The revision removes unnecessary language and highlights the action.

Another example appears when writers describe relationships between objects.

The manager *of the department of research* approved the proposal.

The sentence contains two prepositional phrases that slow the reader. A clearer sentence reduces the structure.

The research department manager approved the proposal.

The revision replaces the chain of phrases with a more direct expression.

Prepositional phrases sometimes accumulate when writers attempt to describe several details at once. When this happens, the sentence may become difficult to read.

Recognizing prepositional overload requires careful attention during editing. Writers should examine sentences that contain several prepositions and ask whether the structure can be simplified.

One useful strategy is to count the prepositions in a sentence. If a sentence contains many words such as *of, in, for,* or *with*, the writer should consider whether some of those phrases can disappear.

This does not mean that all prepositional phrases are unnecessary. Many sentences require them to describe relationships accurately. The goal is to remove phrases that do not contribute essential meaning.

Clear writing often depends on replacing long noun phrases with stronger verbs or simpler structures. When writers reduce the number of prepositional phrases, sentences become easier to follow.

Readers appreciate sentences that move forward smoothly. When unnecessary layers of language disappear, the central idea becomes easier to see.

The next chapter examines another source of unnecessary wording — adverbs that weaken sentences instead of strengthening them.

Chapter Fourteen

CHAPTER 7 & QUIZ ANSWERS

Revise the sentences by reducing unnecessary prepositional phrases.

1. The results of the analysis of the data from the experiment were surprising.
2. The discussion of the proposal in the meeting with the committee lasted two hours.
3. The completion of the project by the team occurred before the deadline.
4. The quality of the design of the system was impressive.
5. The manager of the department of research approved the proposal.
6. The report on the results of the study of the policy was distributed to the committee.
7. The meeting in the conference room on the third floor of the building lasted two hours.
8. The development of the proposal by the members of the committee required revisions.
9. The analysis of the results of the experiment revealed several problems.

10. The review of the proposal by the board occurred during the meeting.

Chapter 7 Quiz Answers

1. The experimental data produced surprising results.
2. The committee discussed the proposal for two hours.
3. The team completed the project before the deadline.
4. The system design was impressive.
5. The research department manager approved the proposal.
6. The committee received the report on the policy study results.
7. The meeting in the third floor conference room lasted two hours.
8. The committee members revised the proposal during development.
9. The experiment revealed several problems.
10. The board reviewed the proposal during the meeting.

Chapter Fifteen

ADVERBS THAT WEAKEN WRITING

Adverbs often appear in sentences because writers want to add emphasis or description. Many adverbs perform useful work, but others weaken writing by repeating information already contained in the verb or by substituting for a stronger word.

The most common adverbs end in *-ly*. Words such as *quickly, carefully, suddenly, clearly,* and *really* appear frequently in both speech and writing. In some situations these words are necessary, but in many cases they add little meaning.

Consider the following sentence.

The manager spoke *angrily* to the staff.

The adverb *angrily* attempts to describe how the manager spoke. Sometimes the context of the sentence already makes the emotion clear. If the surrounding details show that the manager was upset, the adverb may not be necessary.

Another example appears in the sentence.

The runner moved *quickly* across the field.

The adverb *quickly* may not be necessary if the verb itself already implies speed. In many cases the sentence becomes stronger when the verb carries the meaning.

The runner raced across the field.

The revision removes the adverb and replaces the verb with a more precise word. Adverbs often appear because the verb in the sentence is weak. Writers sometimes attach an adverb to a general verb such as *walked, said,* or *went* when a more precise verb would communicate the idea more clearly.

She walked *slowly* toward the door.

The adverb *slowly* modifies the verb walked. A clearer sentence might replace the verb and remove the adverb.

She *crept* toward the door.

The revision expresses the action more vividly without additional words. Another example shows how adverbs sometimes repeat the meaning of the verb.

He whispered *quietly*.

The verb whispered already implies quiet speech. The adverb *quietly* repeats the meaning and therefore adds no useful information. The sentence becomes stronger when the unnecessary adverb disappears.

He whispered.

Writers also use adverbs such as *very* or *extremely* when they want to intensify an adjective. These words often weaken the sentence because they rely on vague emphasis rather than precise description.

The results were *very* important.

The adverb *very* attempts to strengthen the adjective important, but the phrase remains general. A clearer sentence replaces the adjective with a more specific word.

The results were critical.

The revision removes the adverb and replaces the adjective with a stronger alternative.

Another example appears in the phrase *very tired*. The adverb very attempts to intensify the adjective tired. A stronger word communicates the idea more effectively.

Instead of writing *very tired,* you might use the word *exhausted.*

Precise vocabulary often eliminates the need for adverbs. Adverbs also appear when writers attempt to describe emotions in dialogue. Words such as *angrily, happily,* or *sadly* often appear after dialogue tags.

"I cannot believe this," he said *angrily*.

The adverb attempts to describe the speaker's emotion. In many cases the dialogue itself reveals the emotion clearly. Removing the adverb allows the reader to interpret the tone through the words and context.

"I cannot believe this," he said.

If the writer wishes to show anger more clearly, the dialogue itself can express it.

"I cannot believe you did that," he said.

The stronger dialogue eliminates the need for the adverb.

Another common adverb appears in the word *suddenly*. Writers sometimes use this word when introducing an unexpected event.

Consider the following sentence.

The lights *suddenly* went out.

The word *suddenly* attempts to emphasize surprise. In many cases the event itself creates the sense of surprise without the adverb.

The lights went out.

The abrupt statement often produces the same effect.

Adverbs sometimes appear in clusters. Writers may combine several adverbs in an attempt to emphasize a point.

The results were *really very* surprising.

The sentence contains two adverbs that perform the same function. Removing both words produces a clearer statement.

The results were surprising.

The revision communicates the idea more directly.

This does not mean that all adverbs should disappear. Some adverbs perform necessary work. Words such as *carefully, deliberately,* or *unexpectedly* may provide information that the verb alone cannot convey.

. . .

The scientist *carefully* measured the sample.

In this case the adverb *carefully* adds meaningful information about the action. Removing the word might change the meaning of the sentence.

Writers should therefore examine each adverb individually rather than eliminating them automatically.

The key question is whether the adverb contributes information that the reader needs. If the adverb merely repeats the meaning of the verb or intensifies a vague adjective, it probably does not belong in the sentence.

Clear writing favors precise verbs and descriptive nouns rather than vague emphasis. When writers choose accurate words, they rarely need adverbs to support them.

The next chapter examines another pattern that produces unnecessary language — vague modifiers that weaken sentences by replacing precise description.

Chapter Sixteen

CHAPTER 8 & QUIZ ANSWERS

Revise the sentences by removing unnecessary adverbs or replacing them with stronger verbs.

1. The manager spoke angrily to the staff.
2. The runner moved quickly across the field.
3. She walked slowly toward the door.
4. He whispered quietly to the assistant.
5. The results were very important.
6. The worker completed the task carefully and slowly.
7. The report explained the issue very clearly.
8. The child ran very quickly down the street.
9. The results were really very surprising.
10. The scientist carefully measured the sample.

Chapter 8 Quiz Answers

1. The manager rebuked the staff.
2. The runner raced across the field.
3. She crept toward the door.
4. He whispered to the assistant.
5. The results were critical.
6. The worker completed the task carefully.
7. The report explained the issue clearly.
8. The child sprinted down the street.
9. The results were surprising.
10. The scientist measured the sample carefully

Chapter Seventeen

VAGUE WORDS THAT HIDE MEANING

Many sentences contain words that sound descriptive but communicate very little. These words often appear because writers are trying to sound precise, yet the words themselves are vague. When readers encounter vague language, they must guess what the writer intends to say. Writing clearly removes that uncertainty.

Words such as *things, stuff, various, very, numerous,* and *a lot* often appear when writers have not chosen a specific description. These words act as placeholders. They fill space in the sentence, but they don't provide clear information.

Look at the following examples.

The report discusses *various* problems with the system.

The word *various* tells the reader almost nothing. A clearer sentence identifies the problems directly.

The report discusses delays, software failures, and communication errors in the system.

The revision replaces the vague word with concrete information.

Another example appears in the phrase *a lot*. Writers frequently use this phrase when describing quantity.

The team encountered *a lot* of difficulties during the project.

The phrase *a lot* doesn't tell the reader how many difficulties occurred or what kind they were. A clearer sentence replaces the vague phrase with specific information.

The team encountered seven repeated equipment failures during the project.

The revision explains the problem more clearly.

Writers sometimes rely on vague words because they want to keep sentences short. Ironically, vague language often forces the reader to slow down in order to interpret the meaning. Precise language usually improves both clarity and efficiency.

Another vague expression appears in the phrase *some kind of*.

Consider the following sentence.

The system experienced *some kind of* malfunction during testing.

The phrase *some kind of* signals uncertainty. A clearer sentence identifies the problem.

The system experienced a power failure during testing.

The revised sentence communicates the information directly.

Writers also use the word *thing* when they can't think of a more precise term.

The manager discussed several *things* that needed improvement.

The word *things* hides the real meaning of the sentence. A clearer sentence identifies the specific issues.

The manager discussed scheduling problems, communication errors, and missed deadlines.

The revision replaces the vague word with concrete details.

Another vague expression appears in the word *very*. Writers often attach this word to adjectives in order to intensify them.

The results were *very* significant.

The word *very* attempts to strengthen the adjective significant, but it doesn't explain why the results matter. A clearer sentence replaces the phrase with a stronger adjective or additional detail.

The results were decisive.

Another vague phrase appears in the word *several*.

The committee raised *several* concerns about the proposal.

The word *several* suggests quantity but does not specify how many concerns existed. In some situations this level of precision may be acceptable. In other cases you can improve clarity by identifying the concerns.

The committee raised concerns about cost, scheduling, and safety.

In the next chapter, we'll tackle "Repetition That Weakens Writing."

Chapter Eighteen

CHAPTER 9 & QUIZ ANSWERS

Replace vague language with clearer wording.

1. The report discusses various problems with the system.
2. The team encountered a lot of difficulties during the project.
3. The system experienced some kind of malfunction.
4. The manager discussed several things that needed improvement.
5. The results were very significant.
6. The committee raised several concerns about the proposal.
7. The policy created various problems for the organization.
8. The study produced important results.
9. The project involved many different issues.
10. The team addressed several things during the meeting.

Chapter 9 Quiz Answers

1. The report discusses software failures and communication errors in the system.
2. The team encountered scheduling conflicts and equipment failures during the project.
3. The system experienced a power failure.
4. The manager discussed scheduling problems and communication errors.
5. The results were decisive.
6. The committee raised concerns about cost and safety.
7. The policy created staffing shortages and delayed approvals.
8. The study revealed a major increase in efficiency.
9. The project involved budgeting problems and scheduling delays.
10. The team addressed staffing shortages and deadlines during the meeting.

Chapter Nineteen

REPETITION THAT WEAKENS WRITING

Repetition sometimes serves a purpose in writing. You may repeat a key word to emphasize an idea or reinforce a theme. Effective repetition can create rhythm and clarity. Unnecessary repetition, however, weakens writing by restating the same idea without adding meaning.

When an idea is communicated properly, there is no need to repeat the idea — no matter how much you change it.

The following sentences give good examples.

The meeting lasted for two hours *in total duration.*

The phrase *in total duration* repeats information already contained in the words lasted for two hours. Removing the repetition produces a clearer sentence.

The meeting lasted two hours.

The meaning remains unchanged, but the sentence is stronger.

The project was delayed because of unexpected problems *that were not anticipated.*

The phrase unexpected problems already communicates the idea that the problems were not anticipated. The second phrase repeats the same meaning.

The project was delayed because of unexpected problems.

The revised sentence communicates the idea directly.

Another common form of repetition appears when writers use both a noun and a phrase that explains the same noun.

The new policy created confusion among employees who did not understand *the policy*.

The phrase *the policy* appears twice in the same sentence. The repetition adds length without improving clarity. A clearer version removes the repeated phrase.

The new policy created confusion among employees who did not understand it.

Writers sometimes repeat an idea in two consecutive sentences because they want to reinforce a point.

The company experienced financial losses during the quarter. *These losses affected the company's financial performance.*

The second sentence repeats the information already expressed in the first sentence. Removing the repetition produces a stronger paragraph.

The company experienced financial losses during the quarter.

The shorter version gives plenty of information; no more is necessary.

The manager *returned back* to the office after the meeting.

The phrase *returned back* repeats the same idea because the verb *returned* already includes the meaning of back.

The manager returned to the office after the meeting.

The revision expresses the idea more efficiently.

Repetition also appears when writers include two descriptive words that communicate the same idea.

The solution was *completely* finished before the deadline.

The adjective finished already implies completion. The adverb completely repeats the same idea.

The solution was finished before the deadline.

Writers sometimes repeat ideas because they are uncertain whether the reader will understand the first explanation. While clarification can be useful, repeating the same statement rarely improves comprehension.

The report summarizes and gives an overview of the results.

Both *summarizes* and *gives an overview* describe the same action. One verb is sufficient.

The report summarizes the results.

Another example appears when writers repeat the subject of the sentence unnecessarily.

The next chapter examines the most important skill in clear writing — systematic editing that removes unnecessary words throughout an entire paragraph.

CHAPTER 10 & QUIZ ANSWERS

Chapter 10 Quiz
  Remove repetition.

1. The meeting lasted for two hours in total duration.
2. The project was delayed because of unexpected problems that were not anticipated.
3. The manager returned back to the office.
4. The solution was completely finished before the deadline.
5. The committee reviewed the proposal and the committee approved the proposal.
6. The software failed because of an unexpected error that no one expected.
7. The report summarizes and gives an overview of the results.
8. The investigation revealed the true facts about the incident.
9. The staff repeated the instructions again.
10. The team collaborated together to solve the problem.

Chapter 10 Quiz Answers

1. The meeting lasted two hours.
2. The project was delayed because of unexpected problems.
3. The manager returned to the office.
4. The solution was finished before the deadline.
5. The committee reviewed and approved the proposal.
6. The software failed because of an unexpected error.
7. The report summarizes the results.
8. The investigation revealed the facts about the incident.
9. The staff repeated the instructions.
10. The team collaborated to solve the problem.

Chapter Twenty-One

ABSOLUTE WORDS

Absolute words make claims that allow no exceptions. Words such as *always, never, all, none, everyone,* and *no one* suggest that something is true in every case.

In some situations, absolute language is accurate. Mathematical statements often use absolutes because the rules allow no exceptions. In most everyday writing, however, absolute words create problems.

Writers often use absolutes when expressing an opinion or describing a pattern. Because exceptions usually exist, the statement becomes weaker instead of stronger. Consider:

Employees *always* resist new policies.

The word *always* suggests that resistance occurs in every case. Readers who know even one exception will question the statement. A clearer version avoids the absolute claim:

Employees often resist new policies.

The revised sentence still communicates the idea but allows for variation. The same problem appears in:

The new system *never* fails.

The word *never* creates a claim that is difficult to defend. A more accurate version:

The new system rarely fails.

Writers sometimes use absolute words for emphasis, but emphasis can damage credibility when the claim is too strong. Readers tend to trust statements that acknowledge the possibility of exceptions.

Absolute words also appear in phrases such as *all employees, every project*, and *no solution*. These expressions can be accurate when the writer truly means every case. In many situations, the writer intends to describe a general pattern rather than an absolute rule.

Editing for absolute language requires a simple question: *Is the statement literally true in every case?* If the answer is no, the sentence may benefit from a more precise word. Words such as *often, usually, many*, or *most* frequently express the idea more accurately. Clear writing favors accuracy over exaggeration. When writers replace unnecessary absolutes with precise language, their statements become more credible.

Non-Gradable Adjectives

Beyond quantifiers and adverbs, there is a second category of absolutes: non-gradable adjectives. These are words whose meanings cannot be modified by adverbs. They are either true or they are not — there is no middle ground, and no degree.

In recent decades, there has been a trend toward using adverbs to "intensify" these words. If the people you're speaking to know anything about the language, you'll sound ridiculous.

Unique has already begun to suffer. How often do you hear someone describe something as "really unique" or "completely unique"? *Unique* means one-of-a-kind. Intensifiers — words like *so, very, extremely* — are not only unnecessary, they are not allowed. If something is unique, it's unique. It is not *very* unique or *really* unique. It's simply unique, and it cannot be compared.

Perfect falls into the same trap. "Absolutely perfect" is heard constantly, even from newscasters. But *perfect* means without flaw. Something is either perfect or it isn't. If it's *almost* perfect, it isn't perfect — it's imperfect. You cannot be more than perfect, so "absolutely perfect" is nonsense.

Complete means whole, having all the pieces or parts. Something is either complete or it isn't. If it's almost complete, it's not complete. You cannot say something is *very* complete or *extremely* complete.

Unless you're Westley from *The Princess Bride*, it's impossible to be *mostly dead*. You're either dead or you aren't.

Things can't be the *most* impossible. They're either impossible — unable to be done — or they're not. If you have five tasks that are impossible, you have five impossible tasks. None are more impossible than the others. Compare this to *difficult*, which *does* vary in degree, so "the most difficult task" is perfectly fine.

Empty allows for no compromise. A box either is or isn't empty. If something is in the box, it isn't empty.

The same reasoning applies to *equal* and *identical*. Two things are either equal or they're not. If they're almost equal, they are unequal.

Fatal, *immortal*, and *infinite* work the same way. It was a fatal blow, or not. The evil overlord is immortal, or not. The universe is infinite, or not.

A useful clue is the prefix. If a word begins with "in-", "im-", or "un-", it is very likely an absolute and non-gradable:

Impossible — It's either possible or it's not.

Imperfect — It's either perfect or it's not.

Unnecessary — It's either necessary or it's not.

Unequal — It's either equal or it's not.

The next time you're tempted to modify an absolute, don't. If you slip up in speech, no one will likely notice. But when you write it, it's permanent. Be specific. It might make the difference between *mostly dead* and *dead*.

The following is not a comprehensive list, but it covers the most commonly misused absolutes.

Table 1

absolute	adequate	alive	ancient
avoidable	awake	best	black
blameless	boiling	broken	central
certain	complete	confirmed	correct
dead	defeated	defective	different
empty	enough	entire	equal
equivalent	eternal	everyday	everything
exact	extinct	faithful	FALSE
fatal	faulty	final	finest
first	flawless	foreign	full
gone	greatest	guiltless	guilty
harmless	hopeless	ideal	identical
immediate	immortal	imperfect	impossible
inaccurate	incomparable	incomplete	incurable
individual	inevitable	inferior	infinite
innocent	invulnerable	irrefutable	irregular
irrevocable	known	lacking	last
literally	malfunctioning	married	missing
mortal	multiple	necessary	needless
obvious	omnipotent	opposite	overheated
perfect	possible	precise	pregnant
premeditated	present	public	pure
rare	redundant	right	secondary
silent	single	spotless	straight
superior	sure	temporary	thorough
total	TRUE	ultimate	unanimous
unavoidable	unblemished	unbroken	unclear
unconditional	undecided	unequal	unimportant
unique	universal	unknown	unlimited
unmarried	unnecessary	unpopular	unquestionable
unsuccessful	valid	vital	void
vulnerable	white	whole	widespread
worst	wrong		

1

The image above shows this table, but it may be difficult to read, so I'm including this.

Column 1 | Column 2 | Column 3 | Column 4
absolute | adequate | alive | ancient
avoidable | awake | best | black

blameless | boiling | broken | central
certain | complete | confirmed | correct
dead | defeated | defective | different
empty | enough | entire | equal
equivalent | eternal | everyday | everything
exact | extinct | faithful | false
fatal | faulty | final | finest
first | flawless | foreign | full
gone | greatest | guiltless | guilty
harmless | hopeless | ideal | identical
immediate | immortal | imperfect | impossible
inaccurate | incomparable | incomplete | incurable
individual | inevitable | inferior | infinite
innocent | invulnerable | irrefutable | irregular
irrevocable | known | lacking | last
literally | malfunctioning | married | missing
mortal | multiple | necessary | needless
obvious | omnipotent | opposite | overheated
perfect | possible | precise | pregnant
premeditated | present | public | pure
rare | redundant | right | secondary
silent | single | spotless | straight
superior | sure | temporary | thorough
total | true | ultimate | unanimous
unavoidable | unblemished | unbroken | unclear
unconditional | undecided | unequal | unimportant
unique | universal | unknown | unlimited
unmarried | unnecessary | unpopular | unquestionable
unsuccessful | valid | vital | void
vulnerable | white | whole | widespread
worst | wrong | |

Chapter Twenty-Two

WHEN MORE WORDS ARE NECESSARY

Much of this book has emphasized removing unnecessary words. That emphasis can create a misunderstanding if it is taken too far. Clear writing does not mean reducing every sentence to the fewest possible words. Some ideas require explanation, context, or detail. In those situations additional language becomes necessary.

The difference lies in purpose. Words that clarify meaning strengthen writing. Words that repeat or delay meaning weaken it. Writers must learn to recognize the difference.

Consider the following sentence.

The committee rejected the proposal.

The sentence is clear but incomplete if the reader needs to understand why the proposal was rejected.

The committee rejected the proposal because it lacked reliable data.

The additional phrase strengthens the sentence because it explains the reason for the decision.

Another example illustrates how detail can improve clarity.

The equipment failed during testing.

The sentence communicates an event, but it leaves an important question unanswered.

The equipment failed during testing because the cooling system malfunctioned.

The additional information clarifies the situation.

Writers sometimes remove too much language during editing. In those cases the sentence may become technically clear but incomplete. Readers may understand the grammar yet remain uncertain about the meaning.

The report caused problems.

The sentence is brief, but the reader does not know what kind of problems occurred.

The report caused scheduling delays for the engineering team.

The added detail helps the reader understand the situation.

Another example shows how explanation can improve accuracy.

The manager changed the policy.

The sentence communicates an action but not its significance.

The manager changed the policy to reduce overtime costs.

The added phrase explains the reason behind the decision.

Writers therefore must balance economy with completeness. Removing unnecessary language improves clarity, but removing essential information creates confusion.

Another situation that requires additional words involves complex ideas. Some arguments depend on careful reasoning or detailed evidence. A sentence that attempts to compress too much information may become difficult to follow.

Consider the following sentence.

The project failed because of equipment delays, staff shortages, budget cuts, and poor communication.

The sentence contains several ideas. In some situations the writer may choose to expand the explanation.

The project failed for several reasons. Equipment deliveries arrived late, the staff lacked sufficient support, the budget was reduced during development, and communication between departments was inconsistent.

The expanded version allows each factor to appear clearly.

Another example involves instructions or procedures. Clear writing in these situations often requires precise detail.

Consider the following sentence.

Restart the system.

The instruction may be clear to experienced readers but confusing to others.

Restart the system by shutting down the power, waiting thirty seconds, and then pressing the restart button.

The additional words ensure that the reader understands exactly what to do.

Descriptions also benefit from detail when the writer wants the reader to visualize a situation.

Consider the following example.

The building was large.

The adjective large communicates little information.

The building rose ten stories above the street and stretched across an entire city block.

The additional detail creates a clearer image.

These examples illustrate an important principle. The goal of clear writing is not simply to reduce the number of words. The goal is to ensure that every word serves a purpose.

Words that clarify meaning remain. Words that repeat or delay meaning disappear. Writers who understand this principle edit with judgment rather than strict rules. They remove unnecessary phrases while preserving the information the reader needs.

Another useful strategy involves examining the relationship between sentences. Sometimes a writer may shorten one sentence but expand another in order to create balance.

Consider the following example.

The project failed. The team had many problems.

The sentences are brief but vague.

The project failed because the team faced equipment shortages and repeated scheduling delays.

The revision replaces two vague sentences with one clear explanation.

In other situations the writer may divide a long sentence into two shorter ones to improve clarity.

The committee, after having gone through a thorough examination of the proposal in question, came to the realization that there were a number of problems which had an effect on the project's schedule and made it necessary to hold several additional meetings in order to find appropriate solutions.

The sentence contains several ideas competing for attention.

The committee examined the proposal and found several problems. These issues delayed the schedule and required more meetings to fix them.

The revision allows each idea to appear clearly.

Writers who practice careful editing eventually recognize when additional explanation strengthens a passage. They learn to distinguish between necessary detail and unnecessary repetition.

This judgment develops gradually through experience. Writers revise sentences, observe how readers respond, and refine their approach.

Clear writing therefore depends on balance. Economy removes clutter. Detail provides understanding. When writers combine these principles effectively, the result is language that communicates ideas with both precision and completeness.

The final chapter of this book brings together these lessons and reflects on how writers can continue developing clarity throughout their work.

Chapter Twenty-Three

THE VALUE OF SIMPLICITY

Writers often believe that complex language makes writing sound more intelligent.

But sentences filled with elaborate phrases or technical vocabulary can hide the meaning rather than clarify it. Readers may struggle to understand what the writer is trying to say.

Simplicity does not mean reducing ideas to childish language. It means expressing those ideas in a direct and understandable way. Clear writing allows the reader to see the thought immediately.

The organization implemented improvements in the area of communication between departments.

The phrase *in the area of* adds unnecessary structure.

The organization improved communication between departments.

The revision communicates the same idea more clearly.

Another example illustrates how unnecessary complexity can weaken a sentence.

The committee conducted an evaluation of the proposal prior to making a determination regarding its acceptance.

The sentence contains several nouns that hide the verbs.

The committee evaluated the proposal before deciding whether to accept it.

The revision restores the verbs and simplifies the structure. Simplicity also improves rhythm. Sentences that rely on straightforward language often move more smoothly than sentences built from layered phrases.

Consider the following example.

The results of the analysis of the data from the experiment were surprising to the members of the research team.

The sentence contains several prepositional phrases.

The experimental data produced surprising results for the research team.

The revision removes unnecessary structure and improves flow.

Another benefit of simplicity is precision. When writers avoid unnecessary complexity, they are more likely to choose accurate words.

Consider the following sentence.

The project experienced a situation in which there were delays in the delivery of equipment.

The phrase *a situation in which there were* delays the meaning.

Equipment delivery delays slowed the project.

The revision communicates the idea directly.

Simplicity also strengthens emphasis. When unnecessary language disappears, the remaining words carry more weight.

Consider the following sentence.

It should be noted that the report contains several serious errors.

The phrase it should be noted that delays the point.

The report contains several serious errors.

The revision allows the important information to appear immediately.

Another example involves the phrase *with regard to.*

The manager spoke with regard to the changes in policy.

The phrase adds length without improving meaning.

The manager spoke about the policy changes.

The revision expresses the idea clearly.

Writers sometimes worry that simple language will appear unsophisticated. In reality many of the strongest writers rely on simple structures. Their sentences succeed because they communicate ideas clearly.

Readers rarely complain that writing is too easy to understand. They appreciate language that allows them to grasp the meaning quickly. Simplicity also improves the reader's experience across longer passages. Paragraphs built from clear sentences move steadily from one idea to the next. The reader does not need to pause frequently to interpret complicated phrasing.

Consider the following paragraph.

The project encountered difficulties during the development phase because there were problems related to the availability of equipment that was required for the testing process.

The paragraph contains several unnecessary phrases.

Equipment shortages during development delayed testing.

The revision expresses the same idea more efficiently.

Simple writing does not eliminate complexity of thought. Writers may still explain complicated ideas or detailed arguments. The difference lies in how those ideas are expressed.

Instead of layering the language with unnecessary structure, the writer allows the ideas themselves to carry the weight of the passage.

Another advantage of simplicity is durability. Clear sentences remain understandable even when readers encounter them years later. Language built from unnecessary phrases often feels outdated or artificial. Writers who value simplicity therefore focus on meaning rather than decoration. They choose words that reveal the idea instead of hiding it.

This principle applies to every stage of writing. During drafting the writer expresses ideas directly. During revision the writer removes phrases that delay the point.

The result is writing that respects the reader's time and attention.

Simplicity does not weaken writing. It strengthens it.

When sentences express ideas clearly, the reader sees exactly what the writer intends to say.

Chapter Twenty-Four

CLEAR WRITING AND AUTHORITY

Writers often assume that authority comes from complicated language. Academic papers, corporate reports, and government documents frequently contain long sentences filled with formal phrases. Many writers imitate this style because they believe it signals intelligence or expertise.

In reality, authority comes from clarity. Readers trust writing that communicates ideas directly. When sentences become unnecessarily complex, readers may suspect that the writer is hiding uncertainty behind formal language.

Consider the following sentence.

The organization implemented improvements in the area of operational efficiency.

The sentence sounds formal but vague. The phrase *in the area of* adds length without explaining the improvement.

The organization improved its operations.

The revision expresses the idea more clearly.

Another example illustrates how hidden verbs weaken authority.

The committee made a determination regarding the proposal.

The noun *determination* hides the action.

The committee determined the outcome of the proposal.

The revision restores the verb and strengthens the sentence.

Readers respond to clear verbs because they reveal the action of the sentence. When writers rely on abstract nouns instead, the meaning becomes less direct.

Consider the following example.

The company conducted an analysis of the results.

The noun analysis hides the verb.

The company analyzed the results.

The revision presents the action clearly.

Authority also depends on precision. Vague language may suggest that the writer does not fully understand the subject.

The project experienced several issues during development.

The word issues provides little information.

The project experienced equipment failures and scheduling delays during development.

The revision replaces vague language with specific details.

Another pattern that weakens authority involves unnecessary repetition.

The system failed because of an unexpected error that was not anticipated.

The phrase unexpected error already communicates the meaning of not anticipated.

The system failed because of an unexpected error.

The revision removes the repetition and strengthens the statement.

Readers also respond to sentences that reach the point quickly. Weak openings often delay the subject and reduce the impact of the statement.

It is important to recognize that the report contains several errors.

The phrase *it is important to recognize that* delays the meaning.

The report contains several errors.

The revision states the point directly.

Strong writing also avoids unnecessary hedging. Writers sometimes add cautious language because they fear sounding too confident. While caution may be appropriate in some situations, excessive hedging weakens the statement.

It seems possible that the policy may have created some problems.

The sentence contains several layers of uncertainty.

The policy created problems.

The revision expresses the idea clearly.

Of course, writers should remain accurate. If the evidence supports only a limited conclusion, the sentence should reflect that limitation. The problem arises when writers weaken clear statements unnecessarily.

Authority also appears in paragraph structure. Paragraphs built from direct sentences guide the reader through the argument smoothly. When paragraphs contain unnecessary complexity, readers may lose track of the point.

The committee conducted a review of the proposal and engaged in a discussion regarding the potential implications that might arise if the proposal were implemented.

The sentence contains several abstract nouns and unnecessary phrases.

The committee reviewed the proposal and discussed its possible consequences.

The revision clarifies the action.

Writers who value clarity often produce writing that feels confident and persuasive. Their sentences rely on strong verbs, precise nouns, and direct structure. Readers can follow the argument without struggling through complicated phrasing.

This clarity strengthens the writer's credibility. Readers focus on the ideas rather than the language. Another advantage of clear writing is that it prevents misunderstanding. When sentences express ideas directly, readers interpret the message more consistently.

The organization plans to implement changes in the near future.

The phrase in the near future remains vague.

The organization will implement the changes next month.

The revision provides clear information.

Authority therefore depends less on complexity than on accuracy and clarity. Writers demonstrate expertise by explaining ideas clearly rather than hiding them behind elaborate language.

When unnecessary words disappear, the argument becomes stronger.

Readers trust writing that respects their attention and communicates its ideas directly.

Chapter Twenty-Five

A FINAL WORD ON UNNECESSARY WORDS

Throughout this book the same lesson has appeared in different forms. Strong writing depends on clear language, and clear language depends on removing words that do not serve the idea.

Many sentences become weak because writers rely on familiar patterns. They begin with phrases such as *there is* or *it is*. They hide verbs inside nouns such as *decision, discussion,* or *recommendation.* They repeat ideas through expressions like *due to the fact that* or *at this point in time.* They rely on vague words such as *things, issues,* or *various.*

These habits rarely appear because writers intend to weaken their sentences. They appear because those patterns are common in everyday speech and in much formal writing. When writers learn to recognize them, however, the improvement in clarity can be immediate.

Over time this awareness changes the entire writing process. Writers begin to choose stronger verbs during drafting. They avoid vague words before those words reach the final page. Sentences grow clearer because the writer has learned to value precision.

Improvement does not require elaborate vocabulary or complicated structure. In fact, many of the strongest sentences rely on ordinary words arranged in clear patterns.

Clear writing therefore depends on attention rather than ornament. Writers must read their sentences carefully and ask whether each word contributes something useful.

If the answer is *yes*, the word belongs in the sentence.

If the answer is *no*, the word should disappear.

This principle guides every stage of writing. It shapes drafting, revision, and editing. When writers follow it consistently, unnecessary words fade away. What remains is writing that communicates ideas with clarity, precision, and confidence.

Chapter Twenty-Six

WHY UNNECESSARY WORDS PERSIST

If unnecessary words weaken writing so clearly, an obvious question arises. Why do they appear so often? The answer lies in the way language develops through speech, habit, and imitation.

Most writing begins in speech. The patterns we use in conversation influence the sentences we place on the page. Spoken language often contains filler words, repeated ideas, and indirect phrasing. These features help speakers think while talking and allow listeners to follow the flow of conversation.

Writing serves a different purpose. Readers cannot interrupt to ask for clarification, and they cannot hear tone or hesitation. Because of this difference, language that works in conversation often becomes unnecessary in writing.

Consider the following sentence.

I just wanted to reach out and let you know that we are currently reviewing the proposal.

The phrases *just wanted to, reach out,* and *let you know* resemble spoken language. They help soften the statement in conversation, but they add little meaning in writing.

We are reviewing the proposal.

This tells them everything they need to know.

Another reason unnecessary words persist is imitation. Writers often copy the language they see in professional or formal documents. Many business reports, legal texts, and bureaucratic statements contain long phrases that sound official but add little meaning.

The organization implemented improvements in the area of operational efficiency.

The phrase in the area of adds unnecessary structure.

The organization improved its operations.

This repeats a lot of what we've already gone over, but it's worth saying it over.

The next chapter of this book gathers the lessons of clear writing into a single principle that guides every sentence a writer produces.

Chapter Twenty-Seven

THE ONE QUESTION THAT IMPROVES EVERY SENTENCE

Throughout this book many techniques have appeared. Writers have seen how weak verbs hide inside nouns, how phrases such as due to the fact that add unnecessary length, how vague words obscure meaning, and how repetition weakens sentences.

I said before that writers must read their sentences carefully and ask whether each word contributes something useful. But now we get to the real question.

All of our previous lessons ultimately led to one simple question: *Does this word, or phrase, help the reader understand the idea?*

If the answer is *yes*, the word belongs in the sentence.

If the answer is *no*, the word should disappear.

This question provides a reliable guide for nearly every editing decision. It removes the need to memorize endless rules and instead focuses attention on the purpose of language.

Below are sentences that give examples of what we just mentioned. Some of these are repeats of earlier examples, and some may even be exact repeats, but it's worth it to review them again.

There are several factors that contributed to the delays in the project.

The phrase *there are* **does not** help the reader understand the idea.

Several factors delayed the project.

The revision removes the unnecessary opening. It also removes the part about "contributed to" as "several factors" would cover that anyway.

Another example shows how the same question reveals hidden verbs.

The committee made a decision regarding the proposal.

The noun decision hides the action of the sentence.

The committee decided on the proposal.

The revision restores the verb.

The same principle applies to vague words.

The report discusses various issues related to the project.

The word *various* does not help the reader understand the details.

The report discusses scheduling delays and equipment failures related to the project.

The revision provides meaningful information, so this is a case where words needed to be added to the sentence.

The meeting was cancelled *due to the fact that* the speaker was ill.

The phrase adds length without improving understanding.

The meeting was cancelled because the speaker was ill.

The revision communicates the idea directly.

"Due to the fact that" is never needed. Remember that, and any time you see it, you can likely change it to "because."

The same principle helps writers recognize unnecessary openings.

***It is important to note that* the report contains several errors.**

The phrase it is important to note that delays the meaning.

The report contains several errors.

The revision allows the reader to reach the point immediately.

Writers who adopt this question of "does this word add meaning to the sentence" as a habit begin to edit more effectively.

Instead of relying on instinct alone, they evaluate each word according to its purpose. Words that contribute meaning remain. Words that repeat or delay meaning disappear.

This approach simplifies revision. Writers no longer struggle to decide whether a phrase sounds formal enough or complex enough. The only requirement is clarity.

The question also protects necessary detail. Some sentences require additional explanation. When those words help the reader understand the idea, they belong in the sentence. We mentioned this previously, but it's worth mentioning again.

For example.

The equipment failed.

If the reader needs to understand the cause, additional words become useful.

The equipment failed because the cooling system malfunctioned.

The added phrase helps the reader understand the situation.

The same question applies here. Does the phrase help the reader understand the idea.

Because the answer is *yes*, the phrase remains.

Writers who apply this question consistently develop strong habits. They write sentences that move directly toward the point. They avoid phrases that hide the action. They choose words that describe ideas precisely, and readers respond immediately to this clarity.

Clear writing ultimately depends on this discipline.

Every word must justify its presence.

When writers follow that principle, unnecessary language disappears and the idea stands clearly on the page.

Chapter Twenty-Eight

THE WRITER'S FINAL TEST

Every writer eventually faces the same test. After drafting and revising, after examining verbs, removing repetition, and replacing vague words, one question remains.

Is this sentence as clear as it can be?

The test is simple but demanding. It asks the writer to look beyond habit and convenience. Familiar phrases must be questioned. Comfortable structures must be examined. Words that once seemed natural must justify their presence.

Consider the following sentence.

There are several reasons why the proposal failed during the development process.

The phrase *there are* delays the subject. The phrase *development process* adds unnecessary length.

Several factors caused the proposal to fail during development.

The sentence passes the test more easily after revision, and, you saved five words.

Another example reveals how hidden verbs fail the same test.

The committee made a decision regarding the proposal.

The noun decision hides the action.

The committee decided on the proposal.

The revision restores the verb and strengthens the sentence. The sentence is shorter than the previous one, but you still saved two words, *and* you made the sentence stronger and clearer.

Paragraphs must also pass the same test. Each paragraph should guide the reader through one clear idea.

Consider the following paragraph.

The team reviewed the proposal during the meeting. The proposal contained scheduling problems. The meeting lasted three hours. The company plans to expand its offices next year.

The final sentence distracts from the central idea.

During the meeting the team reviewed the proposal and discovered several scheduling problems.

The paragraph becomes clearer.

Writers who apply this test consistently discover that many sentences can improve with small adjustments. A phrase disappears. A verb becomes stronger. A vague word becomes precise.

These changes may seem minor, but their effect accumulates across the page. Readers experience writing that feels confident and direct. They move through the text without struggling through unnecessary language.

Every sentence has faced the same question. Is this as clear as it can be? When the answer is yes, the sentence remains. When the answer is no, revision continues. That discipline defines strong writing.

The writer does not accept language automatically. Every word must prove that it belongs.

When unnecessary words disappear, the meaning stands alone.

Clear.

Direct.

And unmistakable.

Chapter Twenty-Nine

WORDS THAT SHOULD RAISE SUSPICION

Certain words and phrases frequently signal weak or unnecessary language. These words are not always wrong, but they often indicate sentences that deserve closer attention during editing. When writers learn to recognize these warning signs, they can identify problems more quickly and revise their writing more effectively.

We've covered each of these in previous chapters, but let's list them here in one place.

The following categories highlight words that often create trouble in sentences.

Absolute words

Absolute words make claims that allow no exceptions. Words such as *always, never, everyone, no one, all,* and *none* suggest that something is true in every case. In many situations this claim is stronger than the writer intends.

When these words appear, ask whether the statement is literally true in every situation. If exceptions exist, the sentence may benefit from more precise language.

Examples include *always, never, everyone, no one, all, none, every, entirely,* and *completely.*

Filler words

Filler words often appear when writers attempt to add emphasis. In most cases these words contribute little meaning and weaken the sentence.

When these words appear, test the sentence by removing them. If the meaning remains unchanged, the word is probably unnecessary.

Examples include *actually, really, very, quite, basically, rather, somewhat,* and *generally.*

A warning is in order. Many writers have become so accustomed to speaking, and, writing these intensifiers, they view them as important or even necessary. A closer look at the definitions will tell you otherwise.

Vague words

Vague language hides meaning instead of revealing it. Words such as *things, stuff, issues,* and *factors* often appear when writers have not identified the exact idea they want to express.

When these words appear, ask whether a more precise word could replace them.

Examples include *things, stuff, issues, factors, aspects, various, several, many,* and *important.*

Wordy phrases

Some phrases appear frequently in writing even though shorter alternatives exist. These expressions often sound formal, but they rarely improve clarity.

When these phrases appear, consider whether a shorter expression communicates the same idea.

Examples include *in order to, due to the fact that, at this point in time, for the purpose of, in the event that,* and *with regard to.*

The above phrases are almost *never* necessary. If you see them in your writing, they should probably be removed.

Redundant expressions

Redundant expressions combine words that repeat the same meaning. Because these phrases sound familiar, writers often overlook the repetition.

When these expressions appear, remove the word that adds no meaning.

Examples include *return back*, *repeat again*, *combine together*, *end result*, *true fact*, and *final outcome*.

Redundancies should *always* be dealt with. There is no need to have a redundancy in your writing.

Weak verbs that hide stronger ones

Certain verbs frequently appear in phrases that hide stronger verbs. These constructions often create unnecessary length and weaken the action of the sentence.

When these verbs appear, look for the noun that contains the real action and restore the verb form.

Examples include verbs such as *make*, *conduct*, *perform*, *carry out*, and *give*.

Weak sentence openings

Some sentences begin with expressions that delay the subject and weaken the sentence. These openings often add words without adding meaning.

When these patterns appear, consider moving the subject to the beginning of the sentence.

Examples include *there is*, *there are*, *it is*, *it was*, *it should be noted that*, and *it is important to note that*.

Chains of prepositions

Prepositions are necessary in many sentences, but long chains of prepositional phrases can obscure meaning and slow the reader.

When sentences contain several words such as *of*, *in*, *for*, or *with*, examine whether the structure can be simplified.

Repeated ideas

Sometimes a sentence or paragraph explains the same idea more than once. Repetition may occur when writers revise a sentence by adding new words but forget to remove the earlier wording.

When a phrase repeats information already present in the sentence, remove the weaker version and keep the stronger one.

Recognizing these warning signs helps writers edit more efficiently. Instead of examining every sentence equally, writers can focus attention on the places where problems are most likely to appear. When these suspicious words disappear, sentences often become clearer immediately.

Chapter Thirty

SEARCH LIST FOR EDITING

One of the fastest ways to improve a document is to search for words and phrases that frequently signal unnecessary language. Most word processors allow writers to scan an entire document in seconds.

Instead of rereading every sentence carefully, writers can search for common problem words and examine the sentences that contain them.

The words and phrases below often appear in sentences that need revision. Not every occurrence is wrong, but each one deserves attention during editing.

Weak openings

Search for these expressions when they appear near the beginning of a sentence.

there is
there are
there was
there were
it is
it was
it appears that
it seems that
it should be noted that

it is important to note that

Filler words

These words often add emphasis without adding meaning.

actually

really

very

quite

rather

basically

generally

somewhat

sort of

kind of

Wordy phrases

These expressions almost always have shorter alternatives.

in order to

due to the fact that

at this point in time

for the purpose of

in the event that

with regard to

in relation to

in terms of

in the process of

the fact that

Hidden verbs

Search for these verbs because they often appear in phrases that hide stronger verbs.

make

made

conduct

conducted

perform

performed

carry out

carried out

give

gave

Redundant signals

These words frequently appear in redundant expressions.

back

again

completely

totally

final

basic

true

unexpected

past

future

Vague language

These words often hide meaning.

things

stuff

issues

factors

aspects

various

several

many

important

significant

Prepositional overload

Searching for these words can reveal sentences built from long chains of phrases.

of

of the

in the

for the

to the

with the

from the

Absolute words

These words often create claims that are stronger than the evidence supports.

always

never

all

none

everyone

no one

every

entirely

completely

impossible

Common redundancy pairs

Search for these words when they appear together.

return back

repeat again

combine together

join together

final outcome

true fact

past history

end result

These searches do not replace careful editing, but they help writers locate common problems quickly. By scanning a document for these signals, writers can identify sentences that deserve closer attention and revise them more efficiently.

A final note:

Don't get lazy on your editing. I gave you a long list of words and phrases to search for. Take the time and do it. You'll probably be amazed at how many edits you'll make.

Chapter Thirty-One

FINAL EDITING TEST

Revise each sentence to eliminate unnecessary words and improve clarity.

1. At this point in time the committee is currently reviewing the proposal.
2. The manager returned back to the office after lunch.
3. The company conducted an investigation of the accident.
4. The meeting lasted for two hours in total duration.
5. The team made a decision to postpone the project.
6. There are many factors that influence success.
7. The project was delayed because of unexpected problems that were not anticipated.
8. The report discusses various issues that need to be addressed.
9. The board will make a decision tomorrow.
10. The results were actually very surprising.
11. The policy created various problems for the organization.
12. The committee performed an analysis of the available data.
13. The system experienced some kind of malfunction.

14. The proposal was confusing to the staff members who did not understand the proposal.
15. The manager spoke very clearly during the meeting.
16. The discussion of the proposal in the meeting lasted two hours.
17. The report contains several recommendations with regard to safety procedures.
18. The staff carried out an evaluation of the program.
19. The results of the analysis of the experiment were surprising.
20. The committee combined together several reports.
21. The reason why the system failed remains unclear.
22. The team encountered a lot of difficulties during the project.
23. The organization is in the process of implementing a new policy.
24. It is important to note that the results show improvement.
25. The committee reviewed the proposal, and the committee approved the proposal.

Answer Key

1. The committee is reviewing the proposal now.
2. The manager returned to the office after lunch.
3. The company investigated the accident.
4. The meeting lasted two hours.
5. The team decided to postpone the project.
6. Many factors influence success.
7. The project was delayed because of unexpected problems.
8. The report discusses issues that need attention.
9. The board will decide tomorrow.
10. The results were surprising.
11. The policy created staffing problems for the organization.
12. The committee analyzed the available data.
13. The system experienced a malfunction.
14. The proposal confused the staff.
15. The manager explained the issue during the meeting.
16. The committee discussed the proposal for two hours.
17. The report contains several recommendations about safety procedures.
18. The staff evaluated the program.
19. The experiment produced surprising results.
20. The committee combined several reports.
21. The reason the system failed remains unclear.
22. The team encountered scheduling conflicts during the project.
23. The organization is implementing a new policy.
24. The results show improvement.
25. The committee reviewed and approved the proposal.

Chapter Thirty-Two

EDITING CHECKLIST

Another reminder note for editing: Use this checklist when reviewing any paragraph or sentence.

Look for phrases that can be reduced to a single word.

Examples include phrases such as *in order to, due to the fact that, at this point in time,* and *for the purpose of.* These expressions almost always have shorter alternatives.

Look for verbs hidden inside nouns.

Phrases such as *make a decision, conduct an investigation,* and *perform an analysis* usually become stronger when the verb is restored.

Look for repeated time expressions.

Words such as *currently, now,* and phrases such as *at this point in time* often appear together. One expression is usually enough.

. . .

Look for introductory phrases that add no meaning.

Expressions such as *it is important to note that* and *it should be noted that* often delay the real idea of the sentence.

Look for phrases that repeat the same idea.

If two phrases express the same information, keep the stronger one and remove the other.

Editing Checklist: Redundant Words

Check sentences for words that repeat the same meaning.

Common examples include phrases such as *advance planning, end result, past history*, and *true fact*. In each case one word already contains the meaning of the other.

Look for verbs that already include the meaning of the following word.

Examples include phrases such as *return back, repeat again, combine together*, and *join together*.

Watch for adjectives that restate the meaning of the noun.

Examples include phrases such as *unexpected surprise, basic fundamentals*, and *final outcome*.

Look for phrases that duplicate the idea of completion.

Expressions such as *completely finished* or *fully completed* usually contain unnecessary repetition.

Editing Checklist: Filler Words

Search for emphasis words that add little meaning.

Common filler words include *actually, really, very, quite, basically,* and *rather*. These words often weaken sentences instead of strengthening them.

Ask whether the sentence would lose meaning if the word disappeared.

If removing the word does not change the meaning, the word is probably unnecessary.

Replace weak combinations with stronger words.

Instead of *very good*, use a more precise adjective such as *excellent* or *effective*.

Check whether the sentence relies on filler words instead of precise language.

Precise nouns and verbs usually eliminate the need for emphasis words.

Editing Checklist: Weak Sentence Openings

Look for sentences that begin with *there is* or *there are*.
These phrases often delay the subject of the sentence.

Look for sentences that begin with *it is* followed by a long clause.

Expressions such as *it is important to note that* usually add unnecessary words.
Move the subject closer to the beginning of the sentence whenever possible.
Strong sentences often reveal the subject and verb early.

Editing Checklist: Nominalizations

Look for nouns formed from verbs.

Common endings include *-tion*, *-ment*, *-ance*, and *-ity*. Examples include *evaluation*, *development*, and *implementation*.

Check whether the noun can become a verb.

Phrases such as *conduct an evaluation* often become *evaluate*.

Look for weak verbs that support abstract nouns.

Words such as *make*, *perform*, *conduct*, and *carry out* often signal hidden verbs.

Restore the verb whenever possible to make the sentence clearer.

Editing Checklist: Prepositional Overload

Count the number of prepositions in long sentences.

Words such as *of*, *in*, *for*, *to*, and *with* often appear in chains.

Look for repeated phrases such as *of the* or *in the*.

Long chains of these phrases often signal unnecessary structure.

Replace noun phrases with verbs.

Sentences become clearer when the action appears in a verb rather than a noun.

Editing Checklist: Absolutes

Check whether the sentence contains absolute words.

Examples include *always*, *never*, *all*, *none*, *everyone*, *no one*, and *completely*.

Ask whether the statement is literally true.

Absolute language can weaken credibility when exceptions exist.

Replace absolute language with more precise wording when necessary.

For example, replace *always* with *often* or *usually* when the statement allows exceptions.

Editing Checklist: Vague Words

Look for vague nouns such as *things*, *stuff*, *issues*, *aspects*, and *factors*.

These words often hide the real meaning of the sentence.

Replace vague expressions with concrete details.

Readers understand writing more easily when they see specific information.

Check whether the sentence relies on general adjectives.

Words such as *important*, *significant*, or *various* may require explanation.

Provide details that show why the idea matters.

Chapter Thirty-Three

MASTER EDITING CHECKLIST

Use this checklist when reviewing any document. Each item highlights a common source of unnecessary language. If a sentence triggers one of these questions, examine it carefully and revise when necessary.

Remove unnecessary words.

Ask whether each word contributes meaning. If a word or phrase does not add information, remove it. Strong sentences allow every word to earn its place.

Replace wordy phrases with shorter alternatives.

Look for expressions such as *in order to, due to the fact that, at this point in time*, and *for the purpose of*. These phrases usually have shorter equivalents.

Look for phrases that can be reduced to a single word.

Examples include phrases such as *in order to, due to the fact that, at this point in time*, and *for the purpose of*. These expressions almost always have shorter alternatives.

Restore verbs that are hidden inside nouns.

Watch for phrases such as *make a decision, conduct an investigation, perform an analysis*, and *carry out an evaluation*. Replace these constructions with stronger verbs such as *decide, investigate, analyze*, and *evaluate*.

Look for repeated time expressions.

Words such as *currently*, *now*, and phrases such as *at this point in time* often appear together. One expression is usually enough.

Look for introductory phrases that add no meaning.

Expressions such as *it is important to note that* and *it should be noted that* often delay the real idea of the sentence.

Remove redundant words.

Look for phrases that repeat the same meaning, such as *return back*, *repeat again*, *final outcome*, *true fact*, and *past history*. Remove the word that adds no information.

Delete filler words that add emphasis but not meaning.

Common examples include *actually*, *really*, *very*, *quite*, *basically*, and *rather*. Test the sentence by removing the word. If the meaning does not change, the word is unnecessary.

Replace vague language with precise wording.

Words such as *things*, *stuff*, *issues*, *factors*, *various*, and *several* often hide the real meaning. Replace them with specific details whenever possible.

Avoid weak sentence openings.

Look for sentences that begin with *there is*, *there are*, *it is*, or *it was*. These openings often delay the real subject. Move the subject closer to the beginning of the sentence.

Reduce chains of prepositional phrases.

Long strings of phrases beginning with *of*, *in*, *for*, or *with* often signal unnecessary structure. Simplify the sentence or replace noun phrases with stronger verbs.

Examine adverbs carefully.

Words ending in *-ly* sometimes repeat information already contained in the verb. If a stronger verb expresses the idea more clearly, remove the adverb.

Question absolute language.

Words such as *always*, *never*, *everyone*, *no one*, *all*, and *none* make claims that allow no exceptions. Replace them with more precise language when exceptions exist.

Remove repeated ideas.

Check whether a sentence or paragraph restates the same idea in different words. Keep the strongest version and remove the rest.

Strengthen verbs and nouns.

Clear writing depends on precise language. Strong verbs and concrete nouns usually eliminate the need for extra words.

Place the subject and verb early in the sentence.

Readers understand sentences more easily when the action appears quickly.

Look for introductory phrases that add no meaning.

Expressions such as *it is important to note that* and *it should be noted that* often delay the real idea of the sentence.

Ask whether the sentence would lose meaning if the word disappeared.

If removing the word does not change the meaning, the word is probably unnecessary.

Read the sentence aloud during revision.

Hearing the rhythm of the sentence often reveals unnecessary words, awkward phrasing, and repeated ideas.

Ensure every sentence serves the reader.

Clear writing respects the reader's attention. When unnecessary language disappears, the message becomes easier to understand.

Chapter Thirty-Four

PLAIN WRITING

This isn't and shouldn't be a part of this book because it doesn't deal with unnecessary words. But it does deal with a similar problem — clear writing. The legal and insurance professions, and now, many more, have long used convoluted language to confuse and mislead people.

Pick up any legal document, or insurance policy proposing coverage, and you'll see what I mean. It is nearly impossible to understand, so most people just sign the papers — which consist of far too many pages of useless words.

Below is a clear demonstration of how dense legal or insurance language can be converted into plain English. Each example shows the **original legal wording first**, followed by a **clearer version that keeps the meaning but removes unnecessary complexity**.

You don't have to read all of these; they're boring as hell, but they do show how the legal and insurance business, in particular, have been deliberately confusing the public for years.

Example 1 — Insurance Coverage Clause
Original (Legalese)
Notwithstanding any provision herein to the contrary, the insurer shall not be liable for any loss or damage arising directly or indirectly

from acts of war, invasion, insurrection, rebellion, or any hostile act by any sovereign power or authority, whether declared or undeclared.

Plain English

The insurer does not cover losses caused by war or similar events, including invasion, rebellion, or hostile acts by a government, whether war is officially declared or not.

Example 2 — Contract Termination

Original (Legalese)

Either party may terminate this Agreement upon providing written notice to the other party no fewer than thirty (30) days prior to the intended date of termination.

Plain English

Either party can end this agreement by giving the other party at least 30 days' written notice.

Example 3 — Liability Limitation

Original (Legalese)

In no event shall the Company be liable for any indirect, incidental, consequential, or punitive damages arising out of or related to the use of the services provided herein

Plain English

The company is not responsible for indirect or secondary damages caused by using its services.

Example 4 — Payment Obligation

Original (Legalese)

Payment shall be remitted within fifteen (15) calendar days following receipt of the invoice unless otherwise agreed to in writing by both parties.

Plain English

Payment must be made within 15 days after receiving the invoice, unless both parties agree in writing to a different arrangement.

. . .

Example 5 — Compliance Clause
Original (Legalese)

The parties hereto agree to comply with all applicable federal, state, and local statutes, regulations, and ordinances in connection with the performance of their obligations under this Agreement.

Plain English

Both parties agree to follow all applicable federal, state, and local laws while carrying out this agreement.

Example 6 — Indemnification
Original (Legalese)

The Client agrees to indemnify, defend, and hold harmless the Company from and against any and all claims, damages, liabilities, costs, and expenses arising out of the Client's misuse of the services.

Plain English

The client agrees to protect the company from any claims, costs, or damages caused by the client's misuse of the services.

———

Here are some longer examples of the same thing.

Example One
Original Legal Language

In the event that the Purchaser fails, neglects, or refuses to remit payment in full for any goods delivered pursuant to this Agreement within thirty (30) days following the date of invoice, the Seller shall be entitled, at its sole discretion and without prejudice to any other rights or remedies available at law or in equity, to suspend further deliveries, terminate this Agreement upon written notice to the Purchaser, and pursue recovery of any outstanding sums, including but not limited to reasonable attorneys' fees, court costs, and expenses incurred in connection with the collection of such unpaid amounts.

Plain English Version

The purchaser must pay each invoice within 30 days. If the purchaser does not pay within that time, the seller may stop delivering goods, end the agreement by giving written notice, and take legal action to collect the unpaid amount. The seller may also recover reasonable attorneys' fees and court costs related to collecting the debt.

Example Two
Original Legal Language

The Tenant shall, throughout the duration of the Lease Term and any extension thereof, maintain the Premises in a clean, safe, and sanitary condition and shall be responsible for any and all maintenance, repair, and replacement required as a result of damage caused by the Tenant, the Tenant's guests, invitees, or agents, ordinary wear and tear excepted, and shall promptly notify the Landlord in writing of any condition that materially affects the habitability or structural integrity of the Premises.

Plain English Version

The tenant must keep the property clean, safe, and sanitary during the lease and any renewal period. The tenant is responsible for repairing damage caused by the tenant or the tenant's guests, except for normal wear and tear. The tenant must also notify the landlord in writing if any condition affects the safety or structure of the property.

Example Three
Original Legal Language

The Company shall not be liable for any loss, damage, delay, or failure in performance arising directly or indirectly from events beyond the Company's reasonable control, including but not limited to acts of God, natural disasters, war, terrorism, labor disputes, governmental orders, interruptions in transportation or utilities, or failures of suppliers or subcontractors to perform their obligations.

Plain English Version

The company is not responsible for losses or delays caused by events outside its reasonable control. These events include natural disasters, war, terrorism, labor disputes, government orders, transportation or utility failures, and failures by suppliers or subcontractors.

Example Four
Original Legal Language

Any dispute, controversy, or claim arising out of or relating to this Agreement, including the breach, termination, or validity thereof, shall be resolved exclusively through binding arbitration administered by the American Arbitration Association in accordance with its Commercial Arbitration Rules, and judgment upon the award rendered by the arbitrator may be entered in any court having jurisdiction thereof.

Plain English Version

Any dispute related to this agreement must be resolved through binding arbitration conducted under the Commercial Arbitration Rules of the American Arbitration Association. The arbitrator's decision may be enforced in any court with proper jurisdiction.

Example Five
Original Legal Language

The Employee acknowledges and agrees that, during the course of employment, the Employee may have access to confidential or proprietary information belonging to the Company, including but not limited to trade secrets, client lists, pricing strategies, business plans, and technical data, and the Employee agrees not to disclose, use, or permit the use of such information for any purpose other than the performance of duties for the Company without the prior written consent of the Company.

Plain English Version

During employment, the employee may be able to access the company's confidential information, including trade secrets, client lists, pricing strategies, business plans, and technical data. The employee may use this information only to perform work for the company and may not disclose it without the company's written permission.

. . .

Example Six
   Original Legal Language
Notwithstanding anything contained herein to the contrary, the Provider reserves the right, upon reasonable notice to the Customer, to modify, suspend, or discontinue any portion of the services provided under this Agreement where such modification is necessary to comply with applicable law, regulatory requirements, or technological changes that materially affect the Provider's ability to continue providing the services as originally contemplated.
   Plain English Version
The provider may change, suspend, or stop part of the service if necessary to comply with the law, regulatory requirements, or technological changes that affect the provider's ability to continue the service. The provider must give the customer reasonable notice before making these changes.

In conclusion, I call on all people to write to their senators and congressional representatives to call for "plain English writing" in all contracts, legal documents, and insurance and medical documents.

Chapter Thirty-Five

FINAL CHAPTER — LIST OF WORDS TO DELETE

Unnecessary Words and Phrases

Clear writing depends on choosing the right word — and just as important, leaving out the wrong ones. Many common words and phrases add nothing. They repeat ideas, weaken statements, or stretch a simple thought into something longer than it needs to be.

This section identifies those words and phrases and shows what to use instead. It is *not* comprehensive, but it contains the most common words that need deleting.

———

Wordy Phrases

These phrases say less than they take to say it.

due to the fact that

Use *because*.

• *He left due to the fact that he was tired.*

• *He left because he was tired.*

in order to

Use *to*.

• *She studied in order to pass the test.*

• *She studied to pass the test.*

in the event that

Use *if*.

• *In the event that it rains, we will cancel.*

• *If it rains, we will cancel.*

for the purpose of

Use *to*.

• *This tool is used for the purpose of cutting metal.*

• *This tool is used to cut metal.*

at this point in time

Use *now*.

• *At this point in time, we cannot proceed.*

• *Now we cannot proceed.*

with regard to / in regard to / with respect to / in reference to

Use *about*.

• *With regard to your request, we agree.*

• *About your request, we agree.*

prior to / subsequent to

Use *before / after*.

• *Prior to the meeting, review the notes.*

• *Before the meeting, review the notes.*

as a result of

Use *because of*.

• *The game was canceled as a result of rain.*

• *The game was canceled because of rain.*

in spite of the fact that

Use *although*.

• *In spite of the fact that he was tired, he continued.*

• *Although he was tired, he continued.*

with the exception of

Use *except*.

• *Everyone attended with the exception of John.*

• *Everyone attended except John.*

———

Redundant Phrases

These phrases repeat themselves. One word does the work of two.

each and every

Use *each* or every.
• *Each and every student passed.*
• *Every student passed.*
any and all
Use *any* or all — whichever fits best.

  • *Any and all complaints will be reviewed.*
  • *Any complaints will be reviewed.*
  • *All complaints will be reviewed.*

past history
Use *history*.
• *His past history is complicated.*
• *His history is complicated.*
future plans
Use *plans*.
• *They discussed future plans.*
• *They discussed plans.*
final outcome / end result
Use *outcome* or *result*.
• *The final outcome was clear.*
• *The outcome was clear.*
basic fundamentals
Use *fundamentals*.
• *He understands the basic fundamentals.*
• *He understands the fundamentals.*
unexpected surprise
Use *surprise*.
• *It was an unexpected surprise.*
• *It was a surprise.*
close proximity
Use *proximity* or *near*.
• *The house is in close proximity to the school.*
• *The house is near the school.*
completely finished
Use *finished*.

- *The project is completely finished.*
- *The project is finished.*

absolutely certain

Use *certain*.

- *She is absolutely certain.*
- *She is certain.*

free gift / added bonus

Use *gift* or *bonus*.

- *They offered a free gift.*
- *They offered a gift.*

(Frozen) ice — Ice is frozen water.

Full (to capacity) — Capacity means the maximum amount. If it is full, it is at capacity.

(Future) plans — Plans are forward-looking by definition. You do not plan the past.

For the full list of redundancies, see chapter five. It may not be all of them, but it's most of them.

———

Weak Filler Words

These words often add tone but not meaning. Use them only when they change the sense.

- actually
- basically
- really
- very
- quite
- rather
- somewhat
- kind of
- sort of
- pretty (as an adverb)
- just
- simply
- clearly
- obviously
- literally (when not literal)

- perhaps
- maybe
- generally
- essentially
- virtually
- largely

Example:

- *He was very tired.*
- *He was exhausted.*

———

Unnecessary Time Words

These often repeat what is already obvious.

currently / presently / at the present time / at this time

- *The company is currently hiring.*
- *The company is hiring.*

Use them only when you must contrast past and present.

———

Vague Quantity Words

These words avoid precision. Use them only when precision is impossible or unimportant.

- many
- several
- various
- numerous
- some
- a number of
- a lot of
- plenty of

Example:

- *Many people disagreed.*
- *Three people disagreed.*
- *Most voters disagreed.*

———

Empty Lead-Ins

These delay the point.

there is / there are

* *There are many problems with the plan.*
* *The plan has many problems.*

it is / it was

* *It is clear that he is wrong.*
* *He is wrong.*

———

Weak Verb Phrases

Replace them with direct verbs.

* make a decision → decide
* make a suggestion → suggest
* make an attempt → attempt
* do an analysis → analyze
* give consideration to → consider
* come to a conclusion → conclude
* has the ability to → can
* is able to → can

Example:

* *She made a decision to leave.*
* *She decided to leave.*

———

Bureaucratic Clutter

These make writing sound formal without making it clear.

* please be advised that
* at your earliest convenience
* pursuant to
* in accordance with
* the undersigned
* herein
* therein
* whereby
* aforementioned

Example:

* *Please be advised that payment is due.*
* *Payment is due.*

———

Final Thought

A word or phrase is unnecessary if it:
• repeats what is already clear
• weakens a direct statement
• replaces precision with vagueness
• uses more words than needed

Special note:

There are a few phrases/expressions that I covered that — while technically correct — are nonetheless, a part of common usage, and not just in language, but writing as well. A few examples follow.

1. Make a decision instead of decide.
2. PIN number instead of PIN
3. ATM machine instead of ATM.

There are a few more examples, but those are for you to decide whether you want to use them or not. I go with the technically correct, but then again, I'm a stickler when it comes to grammar and language.

To wrap it up:

Clear writing is about leaving out what does not belong, and in a few rare cases, it's about adding a few words for clarity.

ACKNOWLEDGMENTS

It is with great honor that I give eternal gratitude to my wife, all four of my grandkids, and my great-grandson. They give me the inspiration to keep going.

ABOUT THE AUTHOR

Giacomo Giammatteo is the author of gritty crime dramas about murder, mystery, and family. He also writes nonfiction books, including the No Mistakes Careers, No Mistakes Publishing, No Mistakes Grammar, and No Mistakes Writing series.

When Giacomo isn't writing, he's helping his wife take care of the animals in their sanctuary. At last count, they had forty-five — eleven dogs, one horse, six cats, and twenty-six pigs.

Oh, and one crazy — and very large — wild boar, who takes walks with Giacomo every day and also happens to be his best buddy.

nomistakespublishing.com
gg@giacomog.com

ALSO BY GIACOMO GIAMMATTEO

And you can buy them on the platform of your choice.

This brings up a thought: With more than eighty books out now, it is becoming difficult to try to update the list at the back of all of them. If you want to know what books I have out, use the link above, which takes you to my website, or download the latest copy of my GG recommended reading list, which is free.

Nonfiction

Careers

No Mistakes Resumes, Book I of No Mistakes Careers

No Mistakes Interviews, Book II of No Mistakes Careers

Grammar

Misused Words, No Mistakes Grammar, Volume I

Misused Words for Business, No Mistakes Grammar, Volume II

More Misused Words, No Mistakes Grammar, Volume III

Visual Grammar (This is a compilation of volumes I–III with a bit of new information added. It also includes pictures and is the world's first visual grammar book)

Misused Words and Then Some, No Mistakes Grammar, Volume V

Simply Put: The Plain English Grammar Guide

How to Capitalize Anything

More Grammar

No Mistakes Grammar Bites, Volume I: Lie, Lay, Laid, and It's and Its

Murder Is Immaculate (coming soon)

Blood Flows South Series

A Bullet for Carlos: A Connie Gianelli Mystery

Finding Family, a Novella

A Bullet from Dominic

The Good Book

The Ranger

Redemption Series

Necessary Decisions: A Gino Cataldi Mystery

Old Wounds

Promises Kept, the Story of Number Two

Premeditated

The Ranger

Rules of Vengeance Series (Fantasy)

Light of Lights (the beginning, a novella)

A Promise of Vengeance

Undeniable Vengeance

Consummate Vengeance

Vengeance Is Mine (2019)

Note: *Light of Lights* is a novella. It's about 100 pages long and sets the stage for the series. The other books in the series are between 650 and 850 pages long.

Other Books

You can always see current and upcoming books on my website.

Fiction

Memories for Sale (mystery/sf)

The Joshua Citadel (SF novella)

Children's Books

No Mistakes Grammar for Kids, Volume I: Much and Many

No Mistakes Grammar for Kids, Volume II: Lie and Lay

No Mistakes Grammar for Kids, Volume III: Bring and Take

No Mistakes Grammar for Kids, Volume IV: "Would've, Should've" and "Your and You're"

No Mistakes Grammar for Kids, Volume V: "There, They're, and Their" and "To, Too, and Two"

Shinobi Goes to School—Life on the Farm for Kids, Volume I

Fiona Gets Caught, Life on the Farm for Kids, Volume II

Coco Gets a Donut, Life on the Farm for Kids, Volume III

Squeak Gets a Home, Life on the Farm for Kids, Volume IV

Biscotti Saves Punch, Life on the Farm for Kids, Volume V

The Adventures of Adalina, Volume I: Adalina and the Five Tiny Bears

Coming Soon

The Adventures of Adalina, Volume II: Adalina and the Underwater Bears

Get on the mailing list, and you'll be notified of release dates and sales.

www.ingramcontent.com/pod-product-compliance
Lightning Source LLC
Chambersburg PA
CBHW050948050726
47592CB00007B/2489